Managing Passive-Aggressive Behavior of Children and Youth at School and Home

Managing Passive-Aggressive Behavior of Children and Youth at School and Home

The Angry Smile

Nicholas J. Long
and
Jody E. Long

pro·ed
An International Publisher

8700 Shoal Creek Boulevard
Austin, Texas 78757-6897
800/897-3202 Fax 800/397-7633
www.proedinc.com

© 2001 by PRO-ED, Inc.
8700 Shoal Creek Boulevard
Austin, Texas 78757-6897
800/897-3202   Fax 800/397-7633
www.proedinc.com

Library of Congress Cataloging-in-Publication Data

Long, Nicholas James, 1929–
    Managing passive-aggressive behavior of children and youth at school and home: the
angry smile / Nicholas J. Long and Jody E. Long.
        p.   cm.
    Includes bibliographical references.
    ISBN 0-89079-873-7 (alk. paper)
    1. Oppositional defiant disorder in children—Popular works.   2. Oppositional defiant
disorder in adolescence—Popular works.   3. Problem children—Education.   4. Problem
youth—Education.   I. Long, Jody.   II. Title.
RJ506.O66 .L66   2001
618.92'89—dc21

                                                                                        2001019616
                                                                                        CIP

This book is designed in Goudy.

Printed in the United States of America

8 9 10   10 09 08 07

To our children:
Warren, Jeffrey, Jennifer, Matthew, and Andrea
Their significant others:
Sheryl, Kathy, Brooks, and Linda
And our grandchildren:
Taylor, Keith, Ryan, Julia, and Kara

They have made our lives enjoyable, zany,
unpredictable, and rewarding.

I was angry with a friend
I told my wrath, my wrath did end.
I was angry with my foe
I told it not, my wrath did grow.

William Blake

Contents

Acknowledgments

We are deeply indebted to our friends and colleagues who have not only encouraged us but have made significant contributions to the content and organization of this book. It could not have been written without the active participation of the graduate students in special education at the American University, Washington, DC, and the seminar participants across the country, who willingly shared their experiences with a passive-aggressive student or family member.

We would specifically like to acknowledge the organizational and computer skills of our daughter, Andrea Janette Long. Jackie and Lynn Shaw read our first draft and were very helpful with suggestions and careful editing. We thank Dr. Patricia Gallegher, professor emeritus at the University of Kansas Medical Center, for her insights into working with learning disabled students who tend to be passive aggressive. We also thank Dr. Mark Krueger, professor at the University of Wisconsin–Milwaukee, for his specific suggestions. Dan and Maxine Rapoport guided us in preparing the manuscript for publication. Anadel Rich, Wendy Nelson, Yvonne Thomson, Dr. Martin Henley, Norman Klotz, and Dr. Mary Beth Klotz also read the manuscript and gave us worthwhile feedback. Finally, we appreciate the professional and supportive efforts of our editors at PRO-ED, Chris Anne Worsham, Martin Wilson, and Debra Berman.

We were fortunate that none of the above contributors were passive-aggressive but instead proactive in helping us complete this book.

The Secret World of Passive Aggression

Procrastination is a friend of ours. Unfortunately, it also is a behavior of people who are passive aggressive. *Managing Passive-Aggressive Behavior of Children and Youth at School and Home: The Angry Smile* was not written on an impulse or on any publisher's deadline. We have been studying the psychology of passive aggression for over 38 years as part of our clinical and educational work with troubled children and youth, anxious staff, and conflicted parents.

Our interest in passive aggression began in 1962 when we moved from Indiana University to Washington, DC, where Nicholas had accepted a position as the director of Hillcrest Children's Center, a psychiatric residential treatment program for children and youth with emotional disorders. We lived on campus and related daily with the students and staff, whom we got to know intimately. The strength of this treatment program was the professional competence of the residential and educational staff and their ability to manage the aggressive and violent outbursts of the troubled children. We often commented on how kind-spirited and therapeutic the staff were and how skilled they were in controlling their own counteraggressive feelings, particularly when the children yelled, cursed, spit, and tried to hit them. It seemed to us that the staff functioned at their very best when the children were behaving at their personal worst. The staff managed to show kindness and tolerance for deviant behavior for all the children, except one 12-year-old student named Jason.

Jason was an exceptionally intelligent, attractive, well-groomed, middle-class student who had a perpetual sarcastic smile on his face. Jason never lost his self-control or showed any explosive behaviors. He never screamed or swore at the staff and at times he was downright pleasant and cooperative. But when Jason decided not to follow some rule or staff direction, he would quietly and systematically become passively oppositional, which would frustrate the staff. Jason also had the rare diagnostic skill of identifying each staff member's Achilles' heel, and behaving in a way to stir up intense counteraggressive feelings in our competent staff. Jason was the one student deemed the most difficult by the staff and the one they most wanted to punish without any feelings of remorse. How was it possible that this quiet, bright, preadolescent boy could cause so much frustration and anger within and among a sophisticated staff? We did not have an answer in 1962, but today the answer is obvious: Jason not only was a troubled boy but also had a classic passive-aggressive personality.

Because of Jason and the staff's unusual reaction, we decided to learn more about the dynamics of passive aggression. A review of the psychiatric literature on passive aggression in 1963 was limited and focused on adults. As a result, we developed ongoing seminars on passive-aggressive child behavior and invited colleagues, parents, and teachers who were interested in this topic. The only requirement to participate was their willingness to discuss and write up their experiences and observations on passive-aggressive child behavior at school and home.

Over subsequent years, we led over 50 seminars on passive aggression around the country, and collected over 1,200 personal examples of passive-aggressive behavior in school and at home. As we analyzed these examples, we realized we were developing a new and exciting theoretical explanation of passive-aggressive child and youth behavior that was significantly helpful to teachers and parents. We also learned why many of our participants were motivated to attend our seminars.

WHAT MOTIVATED ADULTS TO ATTEND OUR SEMINARS

As we talked with our seminar participants, many of them told us they were curious to know if they were teaching or living with an individual who was passive aggressive. The participants also were interested to discover if they were passive aggressive. We said they could get a glimpse of insight by answering the following two general diagnostic questions:

- **Diagnostic Question 1.** Is there a child or an adult in your life who irritates and frustrates you in insignificant and endless ways, so that over time you have a spontaneous urge to choke this person? If a name comes quickly to mind, the chances are you have identified a person with passive-aggressive behavior.

- **Diagnostic Question 2.** Do you get pleasure and satisfaction by consciously thwarting and quietly getting back at others by procrastinating, sulking, forgetting, being intentionally inefficient, plotting hidden revenge, or making yourself passively offensive. If so, you probably have identified yourself as a person with passive-aggressive behavior.

Once the participants' laughter subsided, we became serious and focused on the complexity of teaching and living with passive-aggressive behavior in school and at home. We are grateful to the hundreds of graduate students in special education, teachers, and parents who participated in these seminars. Without their enthusiastic support and examples, this book never would have been written and we would still be wondering why Jason was such a frustrating student for all of us. (*Note:* Since we are studying the passive-aggressive behavior of both children and adolescents at school and home, the generic term *student* will be used to describe them in both settings.)

UNCOVERING THE MYSTERY

Passive-aggressive behavior exists in all civilized cultures and at every socioeconomic level. Passive-aggressive behavior can be observed in most homes and in all schools. Passive aggression is learned behavior and is a subtle and successful way of expressing personal anger toward others in irritating and indirect ways. The student with passive-aggressive behavior has mastered the art of emotional concealment by hiding his or her anger behind a mask of annoying and confusing behaviors, making it difficult for others to see beyond those frustrating behaviors and to identify the underlying feelings of anger.

Over time, all relationships with a student who is passive aggressive will become confusing, discouraging, and dysfunctional. As we listened to teachers and parents recount their reactions to passive-aggressive behavior, we were struck by the fact that these intelligent adults almost always were unaware of the drip-by-drip, hidden and coded message of anger behind the behavior. When asked to describe their feelings toward a student or adult with passive-aggressive behavior, the participants consistently described having multiple and confusing feelings. Although they initially found the person to be covertly pleasant and likable, over time their reaction changed from feelings of comfort to general irritation to near rage. They said their relationship with the person was like riding on a perpetual emotional roller coaster. One week it was pleasant, the next week intolerable. Most significantly, they described how they became upset by this relationship and how, intermittently, they ended up yelling at the person over minor issues. Later, they felt guilty and confused by their unusual outbursts of anger. As one participant said,

> I am a calm and level-headed woman except when I spend any extended time with my sister who is passive aggressive. Then I end up having temper tantrums and feeling guilty about them. What is confusing to me is that I don't have this reaction in my other relationships.

This is not an uncommon reaction to what it is like to relate to a person with passive-aggressive behavior. The majority of teachers and parents involved in daily interactions with students who are passive aggressive ultimately are beaten down by the relationships and end up feeling confused, angry, guilty, and doubtful about the stability of their own mental health. How is it possible for this destructive interpersonal pattern to occur with reasonable teachers and parents? How is it possible for the teachers and parents in a passive-aggressive relationship to end up accepting the blame and responsibility for this dysfunctional relationship? The answer is clear and painful: Intelligent adults are oblivious about the psychology of passive aggression and they are unaware of the anger underlying the student's passive-aggressive behavior and the impact it has on their own subsequent negative feelings and behaviors.

LACK OF PROFESSIONAL INTEREST

The 21st century will see continued growth in the international acceptance and expansion of the electronic superhighway of information. Every aspect of life seems to be studied, reported, and filed onto the World Wide Web. From microanalysis of DNA particles to cosmic evolution, nothing seems too small or too large to escape scientific curiosity and scrutiny. Nothing, that is, except the study of passive aggression: The psychology of passive aggression, unlike the secret Egyptian pyramids, has remained buried and safe from any comprehensive educational study since the beginning of civilization. This bold state-

> The term *passive aggression* is commonly used by educated people to describe the irritating behavior of others, but if they are asked to describe the etiology of passive aggression and its psychological impact on others, they are unable to demonstrate knowledge of the psychology of passive aggression.

ment is supported by a current literature search of the Educational Resource Information Center's (ERIC's) database, the major educational research database of our country. ERIC reviews over 700 professional educational journals yearly for the database.

We ran a literature search on aggression and passive aggression using ERIC's database over a 20-year period, from 1980 to 2000. Because passive-aggressive interactions are common in schools and exist between students and teachers, teachers and administrators, teachers and parents, and students and students, we assumed we would discover a rich history of studies on passive-aggressive behaviors in schools. However, from 1980 to 2000, there were 2,510 professional articles and studies on aggression and only 2 articles and studies on passive aggression in schools. This was a surprising finding. The obvious conclusion from this literature search is that the psychological study of passive aggression has eluded the professional interest of educators. Although passive-aggressive behavior is demonstrated regularly by students, only rarely has it been described in the educational literature. Like the air that is all around us but not noticed until it is polluted, passive aggression is all around us and goes unnoticed even as it pollutes our mental health.

THE NEED TO CLARIFY PSYCHOLOGICAL TERMS

Any attempt to clarify the dynamics of passive aggression needs to begin with a definition of common terms and concepts. Unfortunately, there is ample psychobabble in the literature regarding the definitions and usages of emotional and behavioral terms. This confusion has served to distort the importance of these psychological terms. For example, the difference between the feelings that drive the behavior and the labeling of behavior such as aggression, hostility, and violence has made any reasonable discussion of passive aggression improbable. To clarify this problem, we present the following psychological definitions to eliminate the ambiguity of these terms as we study the psychology of passive aggression.

• **Anger:** Anger is a basic, spontaneous, temporary, internalized, neurophysiological feeling usually triggered by frustration and consciously experienced as an unpleasant personal state. Anger ebbs and flows in our daily lives. Anger is a real, powerful, and natural emotion, but it does not always reflect an accurate perception of the precipitating event.

• **Aggression:** Aggression is one way the feeling of anger is expressed in behavior. Aggression usually is a spontaneous and unplanned act that often takes the form of impulsive behavior. Aggressive behavior is destructive because it aims to depreciate, hurt, or destroy a person or an object. Aggressive behavior at times can be an automatic response to mounting pain and anxiety and is expressed by yelling, cursing, threatening, or hitting others.

- **Hate:** Hate is a focused or laser-beam feeling of anger. Hate is a feeling that always has a specific target in mind. Hate is triggered by feelings of embarrassment, revenge, and prejudice. Hate is like frozen anger that rarely melts. Hate is learned and can be passed on from one generation to the next. Hate can take the form of personal, racial, national, religious, political, or familial hatred.

- **Hostility:** Hostility is a conscious and deliberate behavior motivated by hate and intended to depreciate, hurt, or destroy a person or object. Unlike aggression, the act of hostility does not have to occur immediately; it can take place a day, a week, a month, or even a year later. Hostility is a personal vendetta often motivated by feelings of revenge.

- **Rage:** Rage is the runaway feeling of anger or hate. Rage is the primitive beast within us, which explodes into violent behavior whenever we feel helpless. A rage reaction, or violent behavior, usually occurs when a person's coping skills are stripped away and the person has no other way of responding to an overwhelming situation of psychological or physical threat. Remember, behind the feeling of helplessness lurks the feeling of rage.

- **Violence:** Violence is the destructive behavior through which a person expresses intense feelings of anger and hate that have turned into rage. Violence is like a volcano. It does not target any person. It is out-of-control behavior that erupts and injures everyone in its path. The victims of violence just happen to be in the wrong place at the wrong time.

- **Feelings of Counteraggression:** The feeling of counteraggression is triggered by anger when a person gets stirred up emotionally. Counteraggression occurs when a person interacts with others who are aggressive, hostile, or passive aggressive. By acting on counteraggressive feelings, a person frequently mirrors the behavior of the person who triggered that anger. When reacting to aggression, a person behaves in a counteraggressive way. When reacting to hostility, a person behaves in a counterhostile way. When reacting to passive-aggression, a person behaves in a counter–passive-aggressive way. Like atomic waste, counteraggressive, counterhostile, and counter–passive-aggressive behaviors are toxic. Unless a person learns to manage and dispose of these behaviors in a healthy way, they will end up contaminating his or her well-being. Counteraggressive behaviors can be identified because they are based on "you" messages: "*You* make me mad." "*You* are always so incompetent." "*You* better apologize." "*You* never use your head." Counteraggressive behavior always attacks the personality of the other person and guarantees that interpersonal conflict will escalate.

- **Assertive Behavior:** Assertive behavior is learned behavior that is used to express anger in a verbal, nonblaming, respectful way. Assertive behavior is based on using "I" messages and not "you" messages (e.g., "I want to share with you that I am having difficulty dealing with your lateness. We promised to meet at noon but almost always I have to wait for you at least 30 minutes. By that time I'm upset . . ."). Assertive behavior clearly defines the limits of what a person is willing to do or not do in an interpersonal situation. Assertive behavior is not intended to depreciate or to harm the other person. It is a healthy way of defining the boundaries of one's personal reality. Assertive behavior is an effective way of making friends with one's personal anger so that behavior becomes constructive rather than destructive.

• **Passive Aggression:** Passive-aggressive behavior does not alternate between passive behavior and aggressive behavior, but combines them simultaneously into one behavior that is both conforming and irritating to others. Passive-aggressive behavior is a deliberate and masked way of expressing covert feelings of anger. It involves a variety of behaviors designed to "get back" at another person without the other recognizing the underlying anger. Passive aggression, in the long run, is even more destructive to interpersonal relationships than aggression. The act of aggression is open and painful, but does not last long. The act of passive aggression is covert, insidious, and could last a lifetime. Passive aggression is motivated by a person's fear of expressing anger directly. The passive-aggressive person believes life will only get worse if other people know of his or her anger, so he or she expresses anger indirectly. For example, the passive-aggressive person might veil anger by smiling and saying, "Hey, I'm not angry. It's no big deal. Let's forget about it." The person might rationalize the anger by saying, "Oh, no, I was not being oppositional, I just forgot"; or "I will do it in a minute"; or "I didn't mean to do that"; or "I didn't know what you really wanted me to do." The person might make endless promises to change, which he or she rarely keeps, or might withdraw and sulk. We believe the passive-aggressive person derives genuine secondary pleasure out of frustrating others. For this reason, we call this pattern of behavior "the angry smile." Wetzler (1992), who has written about passive aggression in adults, calls this behavior "sugarcoated hostility." Regardless of the term used, people who are passive aggressive demonstrate many of the following characteristics:

- Denies feelings of anger
- Fears the expression of anger
- Sends hidden, coded, and confused messages when frustrated
- Creates minor but chronic irritation in others
- Is socially cooperative at times
- Procrastinates or carries out tasks inefficiently
- Can be evasive and secretive
- Will not talk about angry feelings but often projects them on others
- Is quietly manipulative and controlling
- Creates a feeling in others of being on an emotional roller coaster
- Causes others to swallow their anger and eventually blow up

A POSITIVE OUTCOME

As we taught our theory of passive aggression to parents and teachers, we were gratified by their quick insight into the psychology of passive aggression and their sense of personal empowerment to deal with passive-aggressive students and family members. These empowered adults no longer felt like confused victims, but acquired the psychological awareness and skills to alter their responses to passive-aggressive behaviors. Many participants commented that their lives became less emotional and more stable. They reported that they were able to identify the anger behind another person's passive-aggressive behavior. Most important, the participants were no longer programmed to fulfill the other person's irrational belief that adults and authority figures are critical, demanding, and at times out of control. We believe you will experience these same feelings of insight and empowerment as you read this book.

Reasons People Behave Passive Aggressively

Passive-aggressive behavior exists in varying degrees, is triggered by different psychological reasons, and ranges from normal to pathological reactions. From our study and experiences, we have identified four reasons why individuals behave passive aggressively in social situations:

1. As a situational and atypical response to unreasonable adult demands
2. As a developmental stage
3. As a characteristic of a cultural norm or ethnic group
4. As an internalized way of life

REASON 1: PASSIVE-AGGRESSIVE BEHAVIOR AS A SITUATIONAL AND ATYPICAL RESPONSE TO ADULT DEMANDS

All of us have been in social situations where a parent, teacher, or adult makes an unrealistic demand or sets an expectation that we are unwilling or unable to do at the time (e.g., "I want this room cleaned up *now!*" "If your assignment is not in by the end of this class, you will get a zero!"). Instead of expressing our anger openly, we may choose to respond to these demands and expectations in a passive-aggressive manner. For example, we may feign confusion; pretend not to see, hear, or remember the assignment; or behave in ways that will delay and frustrate the standards of the evaluating authority. In these examples, our intent is not to argue with or confront the authority. Our goal is to behave in a socially acceptable way while also defying or getting back at the adult. While these responses are clear examples of passive-aggressive behaviors, they do not represent our only, or our typical, way of responding to frustrating adults and situations. In other situations, we may choose to behave in a manner that is assertive, humorous, aggressive, regressed, dependent, or diplomatic. As healthy individuals we have learned a variety of ways of responding to difficult situations and expressing anger. For us, passive-aggressive behavior is a *personal choice* and not a habitual or predictable response to an authority figure. Our passive-aggressive behavior is a function of the situation and not a function of our basic personality.

REASON 2: PASSIVE-AGGRESSIVE BEHAVIOR AS A DEVELOPMENTAL STAGE OF ADOLESCENCE

Most adolescents go through a predictable stage of passive-aggressive behavior at home by targeting their parents. What parents describe as the irresponsible, lazy, forgetful, and irritating behavior of their adolescent is nothing more than a thinly disguised layer of passive-aggressive behavior.

Developmentally, a typical 16-year-old has achieved close to 100% of his or her height, intellectual potential, and sexuality but only about 20% of his or her economic and personal freedom. A conflict occurs when the adolescent's desire to be free and independent of adult control and supervision runs counter to the realities of life. The adolescent still is dependent on the parents for basic living needs such as room, food, clothing, transportation, education, and money. In addition, the adolescent adds up what he or she perceives as endless discussions or lectures from parents about his or her appearance, manners, language, study habits, grades, chores, music, friends, curfews, drugs, alcohol, dating rules, and use of the family car. Concurrently, many adolescents are reluctant to discuss with parents their long-term academic and vocational goals, as well as their moral and ethical values and standards. Simultaneously, responsible parents often must interfere with their adolescent's immediate plans and pleasures by setting limits on behavior and providing natural consequences for acts of irresponsibility. Given these developmental conditions, a predictable parent–adolescent conflict emerges.

The parents have the manifest power, and they often cast the adolescent into a role of being subservient, compliant, and appreciative. The adolescent's typical response to this situation is to become rebellious or passive aggressive. Most normal adolescents, after testing the rebellion option, end up choosing to become passive aggressive at home. They find passive-aggressive behavior a more satisfying way of frustrating their parents. Adolescents have developed endless and insignificant ways of procrastinating, forgetting, not hearing, and completing their chores at an unacceptable level of performance that drive their parents crazy. Fortunately, adolescent passive-aggressive behavior is a temporary stage that usually exists only at home and not in other areas of the adolescent's life. In Chapter 6 we present actual examples of adolescents using passive-aggressive behavior for getting back at their parents and siblings at home.

REASON 3: PASSIVE-AGGRESSIVE BEHAVIOR AS ONE CHARACTERISTIC OF A CULTURAL NORM OR ETHNIC GROUP

Segments of society have been taught the importance of being socially polite and charming regardless of how they actually feel. One example that may be more apparent in literature and film than in modern-day society is the concept of southern hospitality, which is based on being cordial and congenial in all social situations, and inhibiting and controlling negative and confrontational interactions even when they are merited. Southern hospitality is not earned but is offered freely to all guests or visitors independent of their behavior. Many service professionals, including restaurant workers and salespersons, are expected to demonstrate such hospitable behaviors. When faced with demanding patrons, customers, and citizens, however, these individuals may demonstrate passive-aggressive behaviors.

Some cultures expect children to show respect for their elders and authority figures. For example, many Asian cultures teach their children to honor the status of their elders and to be submissive and obedient to their wishes and demands. If children and youth are upset by the judgments or decisions their elders make, children are taught to swallow their anger and never to debate, argue, or confront their elders. Any overt expression of anger toward one's elders is labeled undesirable and results in losing one's face in the family and community. The suppression of aggression toward elders may create a level of civility and politeness that is admirable. It also creates for some children and youth a reservoir of unexpressed hostile thoughts, a long memory of personal depreciation, and the development of passive-aggressive behavior toward select people at select times.

REASON 4: PASSIVE-AGGRESSIVE PERSONALITY AS A WAY OF LIFE

The development of a passive-aggressive personality is a complex psychological process. It begins with the early, prolonged, and excessive socialization of aggressive feelings and behavior in children. Over time, a child internalizes a characteristic way of perceiving, thinking, feeling, and behaving during times of anger, which ultimately results in the development of a passive-aggressive personality. This unique way a child organizes his or her world becomes the child's psychological character or personal style of relating to others during most stressful situations. The passive-aggressive child has learned that it is safer to express personal feelings of anger and hostility by putting on a social mask that hides his or her true intentions. As a result, the passive-aggressive child learns to disguise anger through indirect and subtle behaviors as an effective way of getting back at others. The ultimate goals of a passive-aggressive child are to behave in a systematic way that

1. Wears the adult down psychologically

2. Frustrates the adult, who then loses control and has a brief, explosive temper tantrum

3. Causes the adult to feel guilty for being so emotional and aggressive

4. Causes the adult to apologize to the child for overreacting to the passive-aggressive behavior in an emotional and unacceptable manner

In this book, we focus on this fourth reason, the development of a passive-aggressive personality in students.

Becoming Passive Aggressive

As we talked with adults who have passive-aggressive personalities, they described their developmental histories in detail. From these interviews, four different socializing life experiences emerged that seemed to explain why they developed passive-aggressive personalities:

- **Type 1:** As a reaction to early, prolonged, and excessive psychological and physical parental abuse.

- **Type 2:** As a reaction to early, prolonged, and excessive parental standards of goodness, social approval, and guilt.

- **Type 3:** As a reaction to dysfunctional and triangular family dynamics.

- **Type 4:** As a reaction to disabling conditions and failed expectations.

TYPE 1: REACTION TO EARLY, PROLONGED, AND EXCESSIVE PSYCHOLOGICAL AND PHYSICAL PARENTAL ABUSE

In our society, there is an assumption that the home is a child's primary source of security, nurturing, and protection. The home is a place where parents should teach their children a sense of belonging and trust, independence, self-confidence, competence, and altruism. However, for many children, their homes are not protective environments but emotional nightmares. The number one place where violence occurs in the United States is not in the street but in the home. Domestic violence is the primary source of aggression in our society and includes physical, psychological, and sexual abuse at all socioeconomic levels. Domestic violence can exist with parents who are authoritarian and demanding, parents who are alcoholic or drug users, parents who have a short emotional fuse and hot temper, parents who are mentally ill or sadistic, and parents who are members of select religious cults. Often these children have watched their mothers or siblings being battered and abused. The children have been threatened, hit, punished, and made to feel guilty over normal, developmental issues. When their parents lose control and act in primitive, aggressive ways, a chronic state of anxiety and fear develops in these children. These troubled parents not only have given up their role as reasonable, caring adults, but also in some cases have exposed their children to inconceivable levels of brutality and hostility.

In our work at a mental health center for severely disturbed children and youth, troubled children shared with us their experiences and fears of parental aggression at home. We provide a few of their painful stories.

▶ **Twelve-Year-Old Tyrone**

Tyrone told us how he had observed his mother being beaten by his alcoholic father to the point that she was bleeding and pleading for him to stop. Afterward, the father took Tyrone into his bedroom and made Tyrone promise he would never tell anyone about what he had seen. The father said this was a private family secret, and he would cut off Tyrone's genitals if he broke this code of silence.

▶ **Nine-Year-Old Misty**

Misty reported she had to get on her knees and kneel in a corner for 3 hours to repent for swearing at her brother. Her parents said this was an evil deed that needed to be punished. Misty reported that this type of punishment happened frequently in her home.

▶ **Eleven-Year-Old Cyril**

Cyril reported that his mother was on drugs and in "one of her crazy and frightening rages." She cut up his clothes because he did not pick up his room on time.

▶ **Thirteen-Year-Old Erica**

Erica, an abused adolescent, admitted to her social worker that her mother's boyfriend had fondled and kissed her over many months when he found her alone. Last week when her mother was shopping, he took her to the basement cot and raped her.

These are only a few illustrations of cases in which children have experienced traumatic abuse by their parents or other adults within their homes. As these children continue to be exposed to the aggressive and unpredictable behavior of their parents, they often learn to identify with their aggressor and become aggressive youth or they learn to survive in their volatile, hostile world by developing a passive-aggressive personality. Just like a child learns not to put his hands on a hot stove, these traumatized children learn not to express their angry feelings out loud to hostile adults. Many abused children conclude that if they show their anger or retaliate, this will lead to further punishment by their parents. These children recognize their feelings of helplessness and lack of power with their dangerous parents. One solution for them is to control their counteraggressive behavior toward their parents, which only serves to fuel their hostile thoughts. They often say to themselves such statements as the following:

- "I can't get back at you now, but I will find a way. And when I do you won't even know about it."

- "You will regret treating me this way. I will have my revenge, and I will enjoy every minute of it."

- "You may think I am subservient and your victim, but I will use all of my intelligence to get back at you."

One psychological truism is that nothing grows stronger or becomes more powerful than an unexpressed hostile thought toward others over time. Many abused, deprived, and exploited children learn this way of surviving with angry and hostile adults. Unfortunately, this pattern of reacting to the angry adults frequently spills over to other adults, independent of their behavior. Once a passive-aggressive child perceives an authority figure as hostile, regardless of whether the perception is accurate or inaccurate, the child will react as if the adult were the abusive parent. As these children grow up, they frequently carry over this passive-aggressive personality pattern into their marriages and social situations.

> The socializing force underlying a Type 1 passive-aggressive personality is early, prolonged, and excessive psychological and physical abuse resulting in the expression of hidden anger based on fear.

TYPE 2: REACTION TO EARLY, PROLONGED, AND EXCESSIVE PARENTAL STANDARDS OF GOODNESS, SOCIAL APPROVAL, AND GUILT

One pattern of early life experiences that promotes the development of a passive-aggressive personality may seem paradoxical because this pattern involves caring and overinvolved parents who love their children and want them to be socially and professionally successful. These parents may have strong religious beliefs, a high need for social approval, and a desire for their children to benefit from all their hard work and financial sacrifices. These parents have achieved the growing benefits of a middle-class life and hope their children will go beyond them socially, professionally, and economically. They want their children to be well behaved and accepted by their friends, teachers, and future employers. They want their children to be mature, charming, well mannered, and polite in all situations because they believe good behavior will enhance their children's chances to make good grades, develop important friendships, win scholarships, and attain a successful professional career.

For example, we attended a dinner at the home of a friend who had a 4-year-old boy who was asked to say grace before the meal. He bowed his head and gave a very succinct and impressive prayer. All the adults said, "Isn't he wonderful?" They turned to his parents and asked, "How did you do this? I can't even get our kids to hold their hands together." These parents enjoyed the lavish praise they received from their friends and likely believe that good parents have good children, and bad parents have bad children. They believe their children are a direct extension of their own values, standards, and beliefs. If their children turn out to be "good children," then they can take pride in their parenting skills.

To achieve what they consider a successful outcome, some parents feel they must be actively involved in the social training of their children. Moreover, they teach their children that good children are always nice, cooperative, obedient, and never angry. Good children have pleasant thoughts and behaviors. Good children are never hostile, sarcastic, or ill mannered. Good children never yell, think, or speak in negative terms. This goal of goodness cannot be attained unless the parents spend endless hours teaching their child to suppress his or her angry feelings.

Specifically, these parents teach their children that feelings of anger cannot be allowed to coexist in their thoughts and actions as a normal, natural response to life's frustrations. For these children, anger is a learned taboo feeling. These parents are effective not only at inhibiting their children's angry feelings and aggressive behaviors but also at teaching them that their angry thoughts must be controlled. Without the parents' awareness, this process of developing "proper and well-behaved children" results in a grievous form of mind control. In the process, their children learn they must not express their angry thoughts, and if they do, they will feel guilty about them. These well-intentioned parents are unaware of how their overinvolvement in promoting goodness in their children will encourage the development of passive-aggressive personalities, causing the parents many heartaches in the future.

Common Characteristics of Overinvolved Parents

Typical groups of parents who are likely to become overinvolved in promoting expected standards include the following:

1. Parents who married late in life and have only one child

2. Parents who had difficulty getting pregnant but finally had one child

3. Parents who are making up for one of their children who has died

4. Parents who finally had a child of a particular gender (e.g., if a family had five boys and then a girl, or vice versa, that child frequently receives special attention)

Unconsciously Teaching a Child To Develop a Passive-Aggressive Personality

To illustrate how some overinvolved parents use the socializing forces of goodness, social approval, and guilt to promote the development of a passive-aggressive personality, we highlight the developmental stages of a hypothetical child we call Paul.

▶ **Birth.** Paul's parents are joyful and pleased they have a normal baby. They are looking forward to raising their son properly.

▶ **Age 6–8 Months.** Paul develops his first tooth and begins to explore his world by putting objects in his mouth and biting them. In the process of nursing, Paul bites his mother's breast.

Parent's Reaction: "Paul stop that! That's not nice! That hurts! If you bite me again, I will take away my breast and you'll be sorry. Nice boys never, never bite their mother. Nice boys never bite anyone."

▶ **Age 12–16 Months.** Paul begins to walk and explore his immediate environment. In the process, he becomes frustrated when he cannot do what he desires and reacts by kicking anything that thwarts him.

Parent's Reaction: "Paul, I want you to stop kicking. You can't go through life kicking things. Nice boys don't kick, and you are a nice boy, so stop it!"

▶ **Age 2 Years.** Paul continues to experience the normal frustrations of life, but now when he becomes frustrated, he responds by hitting.

Parent's Reaction: "Paul, hitting others is bad behavior. Good boys don't hit, and good boys never, never hit their mother. That would be awful. You are a good boy, so you must stop hitting. If you continue to hit, mother won't love you, and then you'll feel bad. Besides the other children won't like you if you hit. Remember, really good children don't hit."

Paul's Psychological Thoughts (interpreted into more adult language): "This is difficult for me to do because I've just given up biting and kicking, and hitting comes so naturally to me. But I want and need Mother's love and approval, so I'll try and stop it."

▶ **Age 3 Years.** Paul attends a half-day preschool program and his parents are anxious to make this a positive experience for Paul. They tell him how important it is to do what the teacher says and to get along with the other boys and girls. The mother picks up Paul after the first day and asks anxiously, "How was your day, honey?" Paul looks worried and in effect says, "Mother, I am the only boy in this class who doesn't bite, kick, or hit. It's a jungle in there! Those kids are mean and nasty and you wouldn't like them." Mother interrupts and says, "But you were a good boy, weren't you, Paul?" "Yes," replies Paul, "I was a good boy and the teacher likes me alot." "Well that's wonderful," his mother replies, "I'm very proud of you, so keep it up."

▶ **Two Weeks Later.** Paul comes home looking sad. Mother asks, "What happened, Paul?" He replies, "This boy, Tom, is in my class and he's real bad. I was riding on my tricycle having a good time, and he came up behind me and pushed me off, jumped on it, and rode away. I got mad and chased him. When I caught him, I didn't do any of those mean things. I didn't bite, kick, or hit him. I just grabbed him by my thumb and first finger and turned my hand to the right. Tom let out a yell, and the teacher ran over asking, 'Paul did you pinch, Tom?' I said, 'Yes,' and she said, 'Paul, you don't pinch kids. Good kids don't go around pinching others.'"

▶ **Age 4 Years.** Paul attends an all day nursery school, and Tom continues to be a problem for Paul. Paul comes home teary-eyed, and his father asks what happened. Paul says, "I was sipping my milk, and Tom came up and pushed my head. He made me spill my milk all over the table and laughed. I couldn't stand it. I jumped up and chased him. I knew I couldn't do anything bad, so I did something new, I went 'spwat.' My teacher got mad. She said, 'Paul, did you spit on Tom?' 'Yes, but I didn't do any of those bad things.' The teacher said, 'Paul, no spitting! Good kids don't spit. Spitting is disgusting, and you don't want to be disgusting. Children who spit have no manners and spread germs. I also want you to know there is a health reason for not spitting, and then she went on and on.' "

▶ **Age 5 Years.** Paul now attends public school. Life with Tom has not improved. Paul comes home with torn jeans. Mother asks, "Paul, what happened to you? Are you hurt?" Paul answers, "I was swinging on the playground swing, minding my own business, when Tom came up behind me and pushed me off. I fell to the ground and ripped my pants. I was really mad at him, but I didn't spit or hit him. I just stood in one place and jumped up and down and started shouting. My teacher said, 'Paul, this is no way to behave. You must stop yelling. Nice kids don't yell. Yelling is for 2-year-olds, not 5-year-olds, and it's time you gave up acting like a 2-year-old.' "

▶ **The Next Day.** Paul returns to school and tells the teacher he wants to leave. He says that if he is forced to stay at school, he will run away. The teacher tells him, "Paul, it's against the law to run away from school. You have to go to school whether you like it or not." Paul looks shocked and says, "But, what can I do? Everything I do when I get angry is bad." The teacher smiles and replies, "Paul, you are now at a stage where you can use words to substitute for behavior. You can talk about what is upsetting you rather than acting it out. That's what young people do. You don't have to hit, scream, yell, pinch, or bite. You can talk about your feelings by using words."

▶ **The Following Day.** Paul is building a block tower, and it falls down. He says, "Damn!" The teacher comes over and says, "Paul, I forgot to tell you. There is no swearing, cursing, or alley talk allowed in school. Your parents would be upset if they heard you talk that way. Street kids use this language and even write it on the walls. But we don't want our well-mannered children to repeat these words or even see these words. Proper children do not use alley language, even if they hear adults use it. Paul, you are a wonderful boy, and good boys use good language." Paul says, "Okay, but the next time I get angry, can I say, 'You son of a beechnut gum'? 'You bachelor'? 'You old mother tucker'?" The teacher looks shocked and says, "Paul, I forgot to tell you something important. No verbal substitutions. When you say 'shucks' or 'bachelor,' we know what you're thinking, so you also must have proper thoughts."

Authors' Note: At this developmental stage, there is a significant fork in the road of socialization. There is no debate about the need to control aggressive behavior in children. Parents need to teach children to give up their aggressive behaviors that are triggered by angry feelings. Parents need to teach children not to bite, hit, spit, yell, or run away. Children need to develop some internal controls over their aggressive impulses, drives, and needs. However, what happens at this point in time is more complex.

The goal of healthy socialization is to teach children nonhurtful ways of expressing angry feelings while also acknowledging that their angry feelings are a normal part of life and can be expressed through words and natural activities such as climbing, play acting, painting, and games. Specifically, children need to learn to say yes to the existence of their angry feelings, and to say no to the expression of those angry feelings in hurtful and destructive ways. This form of socialization allows the child to live in both worlds: the external world of reality and the internal world of thoughts and feelings.

In our example of Paul, his parents not only succeeded in controlling Paul's aggressive behavior, which is necessary, but also unintentionally succeeded in controlling Paul's angry thoughts, which promotes the development of passive-aggressive behaviors.

▶ **Age 8 Years.** Paul comes home and says, "I don't think my teacher likes me. He really makes me mad. I hate him and I wish he were dead!" Mother looks alarmed, "No death wishes. If you ever said you hope a person would die and that person did die, you'd feel guilty and terrible. And never, never say that to grandmother."

▶ **Age 9 Years.** Paul and Tom are now in 4th grade. Paul comes home looking sad, and his mother asks what happened in school. Paul says, "You know Tom still bugs me. Today I told him that I hated him. He was staring at me, so I walked over and said, 'Tom, when I first met you I didn't like you. But now that I've known you for 6 years, I have grown to hate you.' The teacher heard me and said, 'Paul, I'm surprised by your cruel comments toward Tom. Well–brought-up boys do not go around hating others. There already is too much hate in this world. Hatred can only stop if we stop it in our heads. So Paul, no more hate, try to have feelings of kindness.'"

▶ **The Next Day.** Paul tells his parents he finally got back at Tom, who has put on some weight. Today Paul greeted him by saying, "Hi, Fatso, how are you doing?" The parents look at each other and say, "Paul, that was not a nice comment. Remember the old saying, 'sticks and stones can break your bones, but words can never hurt you'? It's not true; name-calling is hurtful. You don't like it when people hurt your feelings, so you must never call people hurtful names. Besides, we are so proud of you that you have grown up to be such a nice young man. So, Paul, don't say anything mean to others."

Projection.

Results of This Socialization

Early, prolonged, and excessive socialization around values of goodness, social acceptance, and guilt encourages a child to hide his or her anger by expressing it indirectly in the following three ways.

▶ **1. Projection: The child learns to express anger by blaming others.** Because Paul is unable to acknowledge or feel comfortable with his anger, he manages his anger by attributing it to others in his world. It is easier for him to internalize the belief and say, "This is an angry world and people out there aren't nice to me. They are jealous and mean to me." Instead of saying "I am angry," he projects those feelings onto others and says, "Those kids are really angry, mean, and nasty. Those kids want to fight with me." Psychologically, Paul attributes to others what he is feeling. During social situations he misreads reality and behaves in a way that encourages his peers, teachers, and others to be aggressive toward him, fulfilling his prophecy that "This is an angry world."

▶ **2. Psychosomatic: The child learns to express anger by swallowing it.** The second way of expressing anger is to swallow it or withdraw from it. This results in psychosomatic illnesses such as headaches, fatigue, and ulcers, and is captured by the old medical saying, "When you swallow anger, your stomach keeps count." For example, when Paul becomes angry, he is likely to become ill and to avoid any confrontation with others by withdrawing from stressful social situations.

Psychosomatic.

The angry smile.

▶ **3. The angry smile: The child learns to express anger by becoming a passive-aggressive personality.**

The socializing forces of a Type 2 passive-aggressive personality are based on adult-imposed middle-class standards of goodness, social approval, and guilt over having angry thoughts.

TYPE 3: REACTION TO DYSFUNCTIONAL AND TRIANGULAR FAMILY DYNAMICS

The third type of passive-aggressive personality develops from the dynamics of a dysfunctional, triangular family. Although these families may differ in age, background, and tolerance for each other, the parents commonly are upward-striving middle-class professionals who assume destructive interpersonal roles. We describe one family in which the son has become a Type 3 passive-aggressive personality.

▶ **Father** is hard-driving, professionally successful, well educated, and well organized, the typical Type A personality. He handles many responsibilities and stressful situations easily. He is a self-directed man motivated by the results of his efforts. He is extremely intelligent and skilled socially. He is perceived by his colleagues as competent and has very high expectations and standards for himself and everyone around him. His relationships with his family members are marginal, although he provides for them materially. The family does not lack material resources. Father tends to be unhappy with his marriage because he perceives his wife to be passive and too dependent.

▶ **Mother** is bright, attractive, quiet, and subservient to her husband. She does not have an independent career and has low self-esteem, although she does have a college degree. She is viewed as socially reticent. She is unhappy with her husband because of the pressure he creates in the family. She reports there is too much stress in their lives, and it is impossible for her to keep up with all the responsibilities. The way she relates to her husband is by being passive aggressive and nonconfrontational. Moreover, she may be a closet-drinker as an escape from the loneliness and frustration of her marriage.

▶ **Son** is bright, perceptive, and overvalued by his parents. He is self-centered and narcissistic, seeing himself as intelligent and in competition with his father. Within the family, he is emotionally involved in supporting and defending his mother, whom he feels is unnecessarily depreciated by his father. Without any verbal discussion, an emotional contract develops between the mother and son. The son agrees to take on and get back at the powerful father by becoming passive aggressive and self-destructive. He knows exactly what the father values and expects of him, so he systematically frustrates his dad in these valued areas.

This family's pattern is typical of families with dysfunctional, triangular dynamics. The son is academically gifted, but he fails a high school math class because he refuses to complete an assignment on time. The son tells the father the work is too "stupid" and to do it would be an insult to his intelligence. The father becomes angry and is concerned his son will never get into the "correct" college. This, in turn, feeds into the son's resistance. The son says he is not interested in college and ridicules every attempt to encourage him to attend. In addition, the son frequently chooses to dress in a trendy, cultlike style that irritates his father. The son wears multicolored hair, uses drugs, and participates in an unusual spiritual group. His arrogant demeanor cries, "I don't care. Nothing is important to me," especially in activities in which the father wants him to be successful. The son becomes a master of excuses, promises, good intentions, and disguised insults toward the father.

This family triangle consists of a successful, demanding father; a mother who is subservient but angry; and a son who carries out the mother's wishes in a passive-aggressive, self-destructive way. This leads to endless family conflicts in which the father ends up exploding in enraged confusion at the son over and over and over again. There are no winners in this triangular family dynamic.

> The dynamic of the triangular family is based on the son or daughter who carries the passive-aggressive message to the targeted dominant parent with such determination that the adolescent is willing to sabotage his or her own life to succeed.

The conflict is one of power, based on winning. But, there are no winners in this dysfunctional family because everyone in the family loses.

TYPE 4: REACTION TO A DISABLING CONDITION AND FAILED EXPECTATIONS

We believe that children with disabilities are more likely to develop a passive-aggressive personality than other children. This possibility may explain why some nonaggressive children with disabilities are difficult to teach and frustrating to live with. Our evidence supporting this belief comes from years of clinical and educational work with passive-aggressive students, and hundreds of conversations with directors and principals of special education programs. More important, teachers and parents attending our seminars continue to validate the relationship between some students with disabilities and the development of a passive-aggressive personality. Like Archimedes, who shouted, "Eureka, now I understand!" our participants have made comments such as the following: "Now I understand why I am having such an irritating and discouraging time with Susan. Now her passive-aggressive behavior makes sense to me!" These substantiating comments do not represent hard research data, but they do provide a groundswell of reality support for our Type 4 passive-aggressive personality.

A Word of Caution About Labeling

Before presenting a psychological rationale for the relationship between disabilities and passive-aggressive personality development, a word of caution is warranted. There is considerable professional concern regarding the negative impact of labeling students according to their disability. The prevailing justification, given by the U.S. Department of Education (1999), is that these categories are necessary in order to fund special education programs. This may be true, but labeling also promotes negative stereotypical thinking about these students.

Table 3.1 lists the number and percentage of special education students served in federally supported programs by disability type during the 1997–1998 school year. Any attempt to make sweeping generalizations about these students with disabilities would be naive and inappropriate. Within each of the 13 categories, the degree of disability varies along a continuum from mild to severe. In addition, these students vary in their ability to accept and cope with their disabilities. Moreover, many students may be included in multiple categories or have additional but undiagnosed disabilities. For example, a student with a specific learning disability may also have a behavior disorder and speech impairment, or a student with a speech impairment may have a learning problem and a physical disability. We believe there are more differences among the students in each category than there are differences among the categories of disability. When it comes to examining the behavior of students with disabilities, again they differ significantly in the frequency, intensity, and duration of their behaviors. Consequently, we must be careful to avoid any generalizations about the personality style of any special education student. Like mainstream students, special education students display the full range of personality patterns, from normal healthy personalities to troubled personalities that exhibit defiance, immaturity, dependency, anxiety, depression, or passive aggression.

Our focus in this section is restricted to special education students who are passive aggressive and not special education students in general. Furthermore, we are excluding those students with a disability who were classified as Types 1, 2, and 3, described previously in this chapter. These students would have developed a passive-aggressive personality independent of their disability. Our Type 4 personality is restricted to those students with disabilities for whom the disability and failed expectations are the contributing factors in the development of a passive-aggressive personality.

The Psychological Rationale for Type 4 Passive-Aggressive Personality

Special education students are first and foremost children moving through the normal developmental stages of life. At each stage, there is a major developmental outcome or expectation for the child:

- **0–9 Months:** The development of a basic sense of trust in adults, enabling the infant to bond with the parents.

- **9–24 Months:** The development of dependence in which the toddler learns he will get more of his needs met if he gives up his infantile omnipotence and adjusts to his family routines, rules, and rituals of daily life.

- **24–36 Months:** The development of the stage of individuation in which the child can begin to separate from her parents and initiate new relationships with other adults.

TABLE 3.1

The Number and Percentage of Special Education Students Served in Federally Supported Programs During the 1997–1998 School Year

Type of Disability	Number	Percentile of Distribution
1. Specific Learning Disability	2,726,000	46.2
2. Speech or Language Impairment	1,056,000	17.9
3. Mental Retardation	589,000	10.0
4. Serious Emotional Disturbance	453,000	7.7
5. Hearing Impairment	69,000	1.2
6. Orthopedic Impairment	67,000	1.1
7. Other Health Impairment	190,000	3.2
8. Visual Impairment	25,000	0.4
9. Multiple Disabilities	106,000	1.8
10. Autism/Traumatic Brain Damage	54,000	0.9
11. Development Delay	2,000	0.0
12. Preschool Disabled	564,000	9.6
13. Deaf/Blind	1,000	0.0
All Disabilities	5,902,000	100

Note. From the *National Center for Educational Statistics*, by the U.S. Department of Education, 1999, Washington, DC: Author. Retrieved from the World Wide Web: www.nces.ed.gov/pubs2001/034b.pbs

- **36–60 Months:** The development of individuation and sexual identity in which the child begins to answer the question, "Who Am I?"

- **6–12 Years:** The latency years and the development of self-control skills, a conscience, academic competence, expanding social skills, and same-sex relationships. Students who have not mastered the previous developmental stages successfully often have difficulty meeting the academic and social expectations of teachers and peers.

- **13–18 Years:** The adolescent years. This is a difficult and demanding stage for almost all adolescents and their parents. The adolescent has a mind of his or her own and struggles to become independent from his or her parents, while simultaneously developing a personal set of beliefs and values, sexual identity and sense of intimacy, and career goals in preparation for adulthood.

Given the complexity of the social conditions in our society, all children will likely experience stressful times and personal setbacks as they move through their normal developmental stages. Acknowledging this reality, does a disability create additional stress for children as they move through their stages of development? Does it create another layer of psychological stress? Does the disability make it more difficult to meet the expectations of parents, teachers, and peers? The answers to these questions depend on the child and the situation. We believe, however, that there is a set of psychological conditions that promotes the development of a passive-aggressive personality.

Failed Expectations

Disabilities prevent some students from attaining the developmental goals of each stage within the expected time frame. This is especially true for children with learning disabilities and emotional disorders whose disabilities are not apparent to others. As a result, parents and teachers have normal expectations for these students. When the students have difficulty achieving their developmental goals or the expectations of others, they not only become frustrated by their lack of performance, but also begin to feel inadequate. This sense of inadequacy is not a one-time occurrence but an ongoing problem that has an impact on their fragile self-esteem. For example, some of these children have experienced difficulty bonding with their parents, difficulty sleeping, difficulty separating from their parents, and poor social skills and peer relationships. They often have difficulty concentrating in school and meeting teachers' academic expectations. Over time, they begin to feel different from others and often are seen as being different and difficult by their parents, teachers, and peers. Unfortunately, the adolescent years only exacerbate the situation. The demands and pressures to catch up academically, to prepare for a vocation, to be accepted by their peers, and to become independent, only fuel the students' feelings of incompetence and inadequacy. These students have marginal frustration tolerance around specific tasks, misperceive social interactions with others, have limited attention spans, and have low self-esteem. Their social-emotional needs dominate their behavior and disrupt academic progress and interpersonal relationships. The more difficulty they have at school and home, the more likely they will hear about their lack of success in school and how they have disappointed their parents at home.

What They Hear from Some Parents

First, we offer a word of support for parents of children with disabilities. These parents deserve all the support, encouragement, and skill professionals can provide them. Maintaining a marriage in the 21st century is not an easy accomplishment under the best of circumstances. The pressures to find rewarding work and economic security, to buy a home, to maintain positive marital relations, to care for relatives and family, to monitor one's health, and to plan for the future are time consuming and at times stressful. For many parents, the decision to have a child is based on a belief that the child will be a source of pleasure and personal fulfillment. The baby will strengthen the parents' relationship and make them proud. What happens when this dream does not happen? What happens when the parents discover that their child has a disability and will require additional parental time and effort?

Larry Silver (1992), a child psychiatrist, describes the normal reactions many parents have in this situation. He believes that parents, particularly parents of children with learning disabilities, go through the following three emotional stages (pp. 92–96):

▶ **Denial: There must be a mistake. It can't be true.**

▶ **Anger: Why us? This is not fair.**

▶ **Guilt: It must be my fault.**

He also found that parents who received and were receptive to psychological counseling were able to work through these stages and end up becoming realistic advocates for their child. This would be ideal for all families, but some parents seem to be stuck in the stages of anger and guilt. Over time the stress and responsibility of meeting the expanding needs of their child wears them down. They feel overwhelmed and defeated. During these emotional times, the parents give in to their feelings of helplessness, and their child may hear the following impulsive and depreciating comments:

- "We never should have had children."

- "Why are we being punished?"

- "We never get a break. Our life is one crisis after another."

- "After all we have done for you, I don't understand why you aren't more appreciative."

- "You are not using your brain or meeting your potential."

- "You are lazy and undisciplined and only think of your needs."

- "You think you know everything, so you never listen to others who want to help you."

- "If you had a better attitude, your life would be better."

- "You give up too easily. One frustration, and it's over for you."

- "I'm sick and tired of trying to help you. You are impossible."

- "You put off everything until the last minute, so you will fail."

What They Hear from Some Teachers

Teachers also give students impulsive and deprecating feedback:

- "You are smart, but you are not motivated to learn."

- "You are more interested in fooling around and acting silly with your friends than in doing your assignment."

- "You could learn if you paid attention to my instructions."

- "You overreact to any corrections I make."

- "You seem to enjoy messing up."

- "You seem afraid to try anything new."

- "Whenever you get upset, you withdraw from the activity."

- "You spend too much time doing insignificant things instead of doing the important ones."

- "You always have an excuse for everything."

What They Hear from Some Peers

Peers often fail to be sensitive and compassionate to others, particularly to students who appear different. Some special education students have been teased, humiliated, and scapegoated by their peers, resulting in feelings of rejection and anger. Here is a sampling of some of the names and comments that special education students have heard:

- Retardo
- Weirdo
- Dumbbell
- Geek
- "You don't get it, so get lost."
- "Nobody likes you."

What They Say to Themselves

Children become what they hear others say about them. Children who have received negative feedback know that they have disappointed others and that, no matter how hard they try, they cannot meet others' expectations. They feel that nothing has ever worked for them, and nothing ever will. They feel unappreciated and misunderstood. Life is unfair, and they are angry. But they also are afraid of failure and fear they will make fools of themselves. Over time, they internalize these negative messages and tell themselves they are damaged, deficient, and dysfunctional. These messages become part of their belief system and their self-fulfilling prophecy. When angry, they resent and oppose any attempt to behave at the level expected by others.

The Passive-Aggressive Alternative

According to Smith (1992), students with disabilities may learn to wear many psychological masks to protect themselves from their feelings of inadequacy, the fear and humiliation of school failure, and peer rejection. Some solve this problem by hiding behind masks of aggression, dependency, or depression. Others discover the psychological advantages of being passive aggressive. They soon recognize how effective passive-aggressive behavior is in manipulating and controlling adults. This behavior gives them a sense of power to replace their feelings of inadequacy, and allows them to be cleverly oppositional without others recognizing the depth of their underlying anger. Like Jason, described in Chapter 1, students with disabilities who also are passive aggressive are the most frustrating and difficult to teach and help.

> The socializing forces underlying a Type 4 passive-aggressive personality involve a student with a disability who has failed in the eyes of his or her parents and significant adults and thus copes with feelings of inadequacy by becoming a passive-aggressive personality.

Levels of Passive-Aggressive Behavior

Passive-aggressive students have developed a diverse and sophisticated arsenal of guerilla warfare tactics that have allowed them to express aggression and hostility toward others in secretive but successful ways. What they say or do is masked so their anger is not easy to detect, but is frustrating to experience.

After evaluating over 1,200 written examples of passive-aggressive behavior, we concluded that it would be misleading, inaccurate, and naive to group all the passive-aggressive examples under one general label. Just as the criminal justice system defines murder in three degrees, we define passive-aggressive behavior in five degrees or levels, ranging from normal passive-aggressive behaviors that we all use at times to pathological acts of passive aggression (see Figure 4.1).

THE FIVE LEVELS

Level 1: Temporary Compliance
"I'm coming!"

At Level 1, the passive-aggressive student verbally agrees to comply with the request of a parent or teacher, but behaviorally delays or consciously forgets to carry out the request. This is the most common form of passive-aggressive behavior and is readily observed in school and at home. This student does not argue or resist the request of the parent or teacher. She does not become oppositional but chooses not to comply at the moment of the request. Her decision to delay or to forget the request may be due to a variety of reasons. She may be involved in some other interesting activity and does not want to stop, or she may be demonstrating adolescent independence. Perhaps she believes the request is dumb or inappropriate or is convinced that compliance will only expose her personal inadequacies. Furthermore, she might be upset with the requesting adult and does not wish to please the adult at this time. It is this last reason, an underlying feeling of irritation toward the requesting adult, that defines the behavior as passive aggressive.

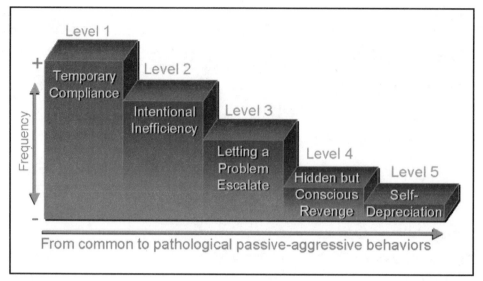

FIGURE 4.1. The five levels of passive-aggressive behavior. *Note.* From *The Angry Smile: Understanding and Managing Passive Aggressive Behavior of Students and Staff,* by N. J. Long, October 1998, paper presented at the Conflict Cycle Paradigm, KidsPeace National Center for Kids in Crisis, 16th National Conference, Allendale, PA. Copyright 1998 by KidsPeace. Reprinted with permission.

Level 2: Intentional Inefficiency
"I'll do it my way."

Level 2 is a more sophisticated form of passive-aggressive behavior. Examples of intentional inefficiency include handing in an assignment that is incomplete and doing chores haphazardly. The student at this level complies with the adult's request but carries it out in an unacceptable way that he knows will upset the adult. At Level 2, the student is upset but also feels the pressure from the parent or teacher to carry out this particular lesson or chore immediately. To delay or to debate the request with the adult would be useless. The student's solution is to complete the task but to do it in a way that will not meet the minimum standards of the evaluating adult. As a result, the parent or teacher becomes so upset by the student's level of performance that the adult becomes angry and usually ends up doing the task. In either case, the student has been successful at justifying his behavior while also getting the adult angry. A typical Level 2 statement might be "I don't know why she's so upset, I did what she asked me to do! Her trouble is she wants everything done her way, perfectly."

Level 3: Letting a Problem Escalate
"Oops, I'm sorry it happened."

Level 3 is a more deliberate and serious way of expressing personal anger toward another person by choosing not to share some knowledge when it would prevent a problem. The Level 3 student realizes that by not acting on her knowledge or observation, her teacher or parent, or her sibling or peer, will have an immediate problem. By doing nothing, the student allows the problem to escalate while also enjoying the other person's anguish. Level 3 is more likely to occur at home than at school. For example, the adolescent knows the car needs gas as her mother leaves for a meeting, knows where her sister's missing shoe is, and receives an important phone call for her dad but says or does nothing about it. This passive-aggressive strategy is a guilt-free expression of hostility, since the student can justify her lack of action by voicing several rationalizations, such as these (accompanied by a smile): "I'm sorry, but I thought you knew about it." "I put the information on your desk." "I didn't know you hadn't read it." "That is not my job; I am sorry this happened to you."

Level 4: Hidden but Conscious Revenge
"I'm clever and successful."

The Level 4 student deliberately decides to get back at a teacher, parent, sibling, or peer by maligning his reputation, frustrating his daily life activities, or damaging and stealing objects of importance. All of these hostile acts are achieved without the other person's knowledge. At this level, the student has *hateful thoughts* about a teacher, parent, sibling, or peer and enjoys experiencing the "sweet taste of revenge." The student is aware that the person with whom he is angry has enough power and authority to make his life miserable, so he decides it is not safe to confront the person openly. The Level 4 student often feels he is being mistreated, unappreciated, or discriminated against, so he feels justified to take revenge in a secretive manner. This behavior could include stealing money from a parent's purse or wallet, hiding a teacher's set of keys, puncturing the tire of a peer's car, creating damaging rumors, or planting a virus in the school's computer system.

Level 5: Self-Depreciation or Pathological
Passive-Aggressive Behaviors
"Getting back at you is worth the pain."

The Level 5 student is fixated on getting back at his teacher or parent and will behave outrageously in a variety of offensive and self-destructive ways that lead to personal rejection and alienation. These self-depreciating behaviors are not as conscious as those behaviors at the other four levels and represent a pattern of pathology that will require professional intervention. This level of self-depreciation is illustrated by the gifted student who drops out of school the last semester, the upper–middle-class adolescent who joins a cult and dresses in bizarre and impoverished ways, and the teenager who gains over 20 pounds or becomes anorexic as a way of getting back at her demanding boyfriend or parents.

DISTINGUISHING BETWEEN A PASSIVE-AGGRESSIVE PERSONALITY AND A PERSON WHO USES PASSIVE-AGGRESSIVE BEHAVIORS

Often we are asked, "If I use passive-aggressive behaviors, do I have a passive-aggressive personality?" This is an interesting question to answer. Most individuals fall within the normal range of behavior and have learned a variety of ways of coping with a stressful situation. They may confront it, attack it, or withdraw from it. They may become sarcastic, regressive, humorous, dependent, reflective, or ambivalent. They may become hysterical, rational, or passive aggressive. The obvious conclusion is that they have many ways of responding to frustrating situations, depending on the time, place, and problem. For example, they may behave passive aggressively by using temporary compliance, using intentional inefficiency, or letting a problem escalate. Moreover, under certain conditions, such as betrayal of confidence or discrimination because of race, color, creed, or gender, they may even react with conscious revenge. However, when all of these passive-aggressive behaviors are added together, they represent only a small part of a person's total range of behavior. This is not true for people with passive-aggressive personalities. During stressful situations, they will respond in passive-aggressive ways most of the time. For them, passive aggression is not a choice but a central part of their personality.

Passive-Aggressive Students at School

Public education for students, like the military, is organized as a top–down administrative system. Each member of the school system has a designated rank, responsibility, role, and function. This administrative pecking order in a school system is the standard and accepted way of operating. The superintendent has the most authority and power to manage and control the educational system. The superintendent delegates specific responsibilities to the assistant superintendent, supervisors, principals, teachers, and classroom aides in a descending stair-step order. All of these adults, however, have more power and status than do the students. The students virtually are placed in a powerless and subservient role in many school systems. If students are going to succeed academically in these settings, they must accept their roles as submissive and compliant to the authority of the teacher and his or her classroom values, standards, and rules. Students also must be motivated to learn and have the prerequisite skills to attend class and to respond to the classroom lesson quickly and quietly. Most of all they need to be able to control their daily frustrations in the classroom without becoming behavior problems for the teacher. In our observation of classrooms and in consultation with teachers and principles, the authoritarian or perfectionistic teachers most frequently encourage the development of situational passive-aggressive behavior in students.

THE AUTHORITARIAN TEACHER

The classroom teacher is the primary authority figure for students. He or she has the responsibility of teaching the assigned curriculum and objectives of the grade level. The teacher's personality and the social atmosphere he or she creates in the classroom have a profound influence on students' attitudes, feelings, and behaviors. If the teacher is authoritarian, has perfectionistic and unreasonable standards, focuses on negative student behavior, and actively punishes students who deviate from his or her expectations, the teacher sets the psychological conditions for the students to learn passive-aggressive ways of relating to him or her.

We have observed a few teachers who fit this profile. We also have observed students who are not typically passive aggressive become passive aggressive as a way of coping with a demanding, authoritarian, perfectionistic teacher. In our experience, teachers seem to have little awareness of the dynamics of a passive-aggressive student. They find it irritating and confusing that a nonaggressive student can cause them to experience such feelings of anger over time. Teachers have described how they have "had it" with these students and how they can no longer even look at these students without feeling animosity toward them.

EXAMPLES OF PASSIVE-AGGRESSIVE BEHAVIOR IN THE CLASSROOM

In this section, we describe typical passive-aggressive behaviors used by students in the classroom. Some actual examples were selected to illustrate the successful ways students can frustrate their teachers and teachers can frustrate their students in passive-aggressive ways. The examples were chosen from stories provided by our seminar participants. The discussion is divided into the five levels of passive-aggressive behavior that we discussed in Chapter 4. Passive-aggressive students are not restricted to any one of the tactics described. The skilled passive-aggressive student uses a variety of techniques to get the teacher stirred up emotionally.

Level 1: Temporary Compliance

This level of passive-aggressive behavior occurs when a student is requested by an adult to carry out a specific task that he or she does not want to do at this time. Instead of resisting, he or she agrees to do it, but then delays or does not do it.

Temporary Blindness

Students who are passive aggressive frequently have social myopia or temporary blindness when they do not want to comply with a teacher's request. The pretense is an effective way of expressing one's anger while simultaneously apologizing and saying, "Oh, I'm sorry."

"I can't see it"

Gary is a polite student with a learning disability in my 4th-grade class. When I ask him to do something in class, he rarely says no. Most of the time he agrees to do it but then doesn't do it. One day I asked Gary if he would walk to the bookshelf at the back of the classroom and bring me the encyclopedia lettered M. Gary nodded, but he didn't seem happy. He slowly walked over to the shelf and said, "I don't see it!" I told him that he was looking at the top shelf instead of the middle shelf. He replied, "It's still not here." I asked him if he could find the W, pull it out of the bookcase, and see if it was the M placed upside down. Gary looked for a few minutes, turned and said, "It's not there." By this time I was so frustrated, I walked toward Gary and from about 8 feet away I spotted the M volume. I looked at him in a disgusted way and said, "There it is." He replied, "Oh, I didn't see it!"

Temporary Deafness

If a student is unprepared or is angry with the teacher and is called on in class, a passive-aggressive tactic is to feign deafness and not respond. Many passive-aggressive students have learned the act of deafness—a useful strategy when they do not want to participate—and use it as an enjoyable way of frustrating the teacher.

"Karen, can you hear me?"

Karen is in my 9th-grade math class. She is well behaved and smart but occasionally I have noticed that she seems not to hear me when I call on her. Yesterday I wrote a simple equation on the board. I noted that Karen was not paying attention, so I asked her to solve it. Karen did not respond. So I repeated her name a second time. Still, she did not look up or answer. By this time I was angry and yelled, "Karen!" She looked up and said meekly, "Are you calling me?" "Yes," I replied sternly. Karen smiled, "Oh, I'm sorry. I didn't hear you. What is it you'd like me to do?" I was so upset, I replied, "Just forget it. I'll ask a student who is paying attention."

"I'll take the Fifth Amendment"

Up until the 5th grade, I was a model student and many times the teacher's pet. Then I felt my 5th-grade teacher did not like me, so I disliked her. She always wrote on my report card that I talked too much, was a social butterfly, and never finished my work. I really hated her and couldn't understand why she didn't like me. I remember clearly, I decided I would never talk to her again unless she initiated it. Then, I pretended not to hear her until she asked me twice. I know that my behavior upset her, but what she didn't know was how much I was enjoying not talking to her.

Temporary Brain Damage

A number of students can recall with complete accuracy some specific information, such as the correct statistics of every leading football player in the NFL. But when it comes to carrying out a simple task that they prefer not to do, they will quickly agree to do it and then promptly "forget" to do it. They seem to have episodes of temporary brain damage that interferes with their ability to remember anything they do not want to do. Whether it is returning a book to the school library or signing up for a classroom project, the student seems to forget to do it. When reminded by a teacher, the student is likely to respond, "Oh yes, I'll do it. It slipped my mind." What is frustrating for the teacher is that this type of behavior happens again and again, and the student does not appear to be learning from this experience regardless of the teacher's criticism.

The Art of Procrastination and the Skill of Dawdling

Many passive-aggressive students have perfected the art of procrastination or completing any assigned task with unnecessary slowness. They do not feign temporary blindness, deafness, or brain damage. They agree to do the assigned task but then dawdle, mess around, and delay completing the task as long as possible. The modus operandi seems to be "When upset at the adult, never do anything today that I might consider doing tomorrow." When the teacher confronts them about their behavior, they make endless and emotional promises to make up all of the unfinished work and to complete the assignment. However, they become creative and clever in devising excuses to explain why they were unable to meet their promises. Teaching one of these students can be an irritating experience for teachers.

"If I only had more patience"

I was taking my 6th-grade class to the library. All of the students were in line and ready to go, except Eric, a student who is mainstreamed in my class. Eric was still at his desk, so I said, "Eric, come on. Let's get going!" Eric gave me that classical answer, "I'm coming." I thought that perhaps Eric was mad at me, because earlier that morning I told him to quit goofing around and to attend to his work. Instead of lining up with his class, he started to pick up all of the paper under his desk, behavior that would have been appropriate 10 minutes earlier but was totally inappropriate now. Next, he walked over to the pencil sharpener and began to empty it. By then, I was fuming. Eric was holding up the entire class and I seemed to be tolerating it. Finally I had it and yelled, "Eric, come now! Come this very second!" Eric looked surprised and said, "You know if you would have waited one half of a second more, I was coming. My foot was in the air, so you didn't have to yell at me. I was only trying to clean up." After I took the class to the library, I began to doubt my own ability. Perhaps I should have been more patient. Maybe I should be more tolerant. And maybe I did overreact. After all, Eric *was* cleaning up the classroom.

Level 2: Intentional Inefficiency

Level 2 passive-aggressive behavior occurs when a student is unwilling to do work or is just plain angry with a teacher for some previous incident. The student expresses anger by completing the assigned task in a manner and at a quality level that are certain to upset the teacher. Once again, the student is not being openly resistant to the teacher's request. The student cannot be accused of not doing the assignment. This protects the student from being identified as oppositional while also providing the opportunity to get back at the teacher behind a mask of inefficiency.

"Never help again!"

Mr. Brown asked Myra to water the classroom plants. In the process, Myra managed to knock a plant off the windowsill, spill water on the floor, accidentally hit another pupil with the broom while sweeping up the plant debris, bump into another pupil who was painting, and step on the toes of a shy pupil on her way to the teacher's desk. Finally, Mr. Brown shouted, "Myra, I never want you to help me again!" "Gee, Mr. Brown, I was just trying to do what you wanted me to do and clean up our room," Myra replied.

"I'll never help you again"

I'm a special education teacher and take pride in my ability to reeducate troubled students. For 90% of the students, I am a successful teacher. But when it comes to Todd, nothing seems to work. I can't explain why he upsets me or why I get so frustrated when I try to help him. Yesterday, he made me so angry I walked away from him saying, "Todd, I'm never going to help you again unless you change your attitude." This is not like me. I'm usually more understanding and tolerant of kids' problems. Yesterday, Todd raised his hand and said that he was having some trouble with his math story problems and asked me for help. I said I would be happy to help, and he asked me to read the first problem to him. As I started to read, I noticed that Todd started staring at the ceiling. When I asked him what he was doing, he said that he was staring at the ceiling because it helps him think better. I asked him to do me a favor and to try thinking as he was silently reading the math problem. He replied, "Sure thing, no problem." He asked me to read the same problem a second time, and while I was reading it, Todd was rocking back and forth in his chair. I reached out and put my hand on the back of his chair and said, "Todd, please keep the four legs of your chair on the floor." He replied, "Sure thing, Teach, no problem." He asked me to read the same problem a third time. By now I was getting angry and said, "I want you to pay attention. This is the last time I'm going to read this to you." I read, and Todd started making clicking noises with his tongue while also tapping a pencil on his desk. Finally, I said, "Todd, that's it! I'm not helping you now or in the future, until you pay attention." Todd smirked and said, "But Teach, that's the reason why I'm in your special ed class." As I left him, I felt like tearing out my hair.

The painful hello

Tony was an adolescent in our school who had strong negative feelings toward authority figures, especially me, the principal. Each morning, I walked through the corridors and met the students when the school buses arrived. If Tony saw me, he would come up to me, say "Good morning," and simultaneously punch me on the shoulder. His punch was just hard enough so I knew it wasn't friendship, but it wasn't too hard either. I knew if I tried to call Tony on this behavior, he would say, "Hey, Big Man, I was just trying to be friendly. I don't know why you're making such a big deal out of saying 'hello.'" Thinking about this, I decided to set new boundaries with Tony. I said to him, "I appreciate your wanting to say 'hello' to me, but let's do it in a different way. When you see me, I want you to stop, say 'Good morning,' and stick out your hand. I will stop, say 'Good morning, Tony,' and stick out my hand. Then we will shake hands like gentlemen." I asked him to repeat what I said to make sure we both knew the procedure. The next day, I met Tony in the corridor. He walked over, stopped, and said, "Hello." I stopped and said, "Good morning, Tony." As we were shaking hands, he stepped on my toes. He immediately apologized, but I noticed a small grin on his face. Tony just demonstrated the dynamics of passive-aggressive behavior. We were shaking hands, an act of friendship, while he was stepping on my toes, an act of hostility.

One eye open, one eye closed

Trenton, who has a learning disability, was a member of our school tumbling group. Mr. Spaniel, his gym teacher, had arranged for a special practice session that was scheduled to take place at the same time I was to meet with Trenton for his weekly remedial reading session. This reading session had priorities over other school activities and could not be rescheduled. Trenton did not tell me about his tumbling practice, and I was unaware that Trenton wanted very much to be with his team. When Trenton entered my office, he seemed rather sluggish. On the other hand, I had organized a very exciting and helpful lesson for him. When I gave Trenton the assignment and asked him to read, I was surprised by his behavior. As he started to read, he put his right hand over his right eye. When I asked him why he was doing this, he replied, "I am learning to read with my left eye in case I injure my right eye." I told him to put his hand down and to stop playing around. Trenton looked at me, dropped his right hand, and then put his left hand over his left eye and continued to read. I was so annoyed by his behavior and so disappointed that my wonderful lesson would never be appreciated that I said to him, "Trenton, that's it. No more remedial reading for you. I want you to go back to your class." Trenton grinned and said, "Thank you very much." I didn't understand his behavior until I later learned that he immediately went to his tumbling session.

These examples of passive-aggressive behaviors illustrate some of the many ways students can use intentional inefficiency as a way of getting back at the teacher. There are other methods: Some students have learned to frustrate adults by talking slowly or quietly. The teacher asks them a question, and their reply is so halted and meandering that the teacher says loudly, "Come on, speed it up! Cut to the action!" Or, "Speak a little louder; we can't hear you." Another passive-aggressive tactic is to respond to the teacher's comment in a concrete manner causing the other students to laugh. The teacher says, "I want everyone in this class to be quiet as a mouse." And Johnny replies, "Squeak, squeak, squeak, right?" Or the teacher might say, "Cut it out!" and Melissa says, "Cut, cut, cut, cut, cut," making a scissors motion with her hand. A 3rd-grade teacher reported an incident with Larry when she read a story about farm animals. When she came to the name of an animal, Larry made the sound of that animal. This caused the other students to join him, so Larry was reprimanded. He replied, "I thought I was being helpful and you wanted me to show the class how the animals sounded."

Level 3: Letting a Problem Escalate

In Level 3 passive-aggressive behavior, the student expresses anger at the teacher by making a conscious decision not to act when such action would have prevented the teacher from reacting.

Keys to success

I must have been 13 or 14 years old when this incident happened in my high school art class. I always thought of myself as a better than average art student, and many of my friends would compliment me on how unusual and creative my artwork was. This particular period, Mrs. Brandis was returning our mid-semester art projects, and I was eagerly awaiting my grade. When I looked at my grade, I was upset. I received a C when I was sure I deserved at least a B. I remember thinking that Mrs. Brandis didn't like me and gave me this low grade not because of my art project, but because she thought I was too spunky.

I was still sulking later in the period when I noticed that Mrs. Brandis's set of keys accidentally dropped into an open drawer as she was cleaning up the art table. I knew they were the keys to her kingdom, but I decided not to say anything. At the end of the art period, Mrs. Brandis started looking for her keys. When she couldn't find them, she panicked and asked everyone in the class to look for them. She kept on explaining how important they were and how they must be found. Ten minutes later they were still lost, and Mrs. Brandis was distraught. She said she didn't know what she would do, since she wouldn't be able to drive home, and she had to take care of her elderly mother. Finally, I felt I had enjoyed watching her "stew in her own juices" long enough. I quietly mentioned that the last time I saw her keys they were on the art table. We walked over and she started moving the jars and piles of paper around. I started to open the drawers, and much to my amazement, I found her keys in the third drawer. Mrs. Brandis could not thank me enough. She was most appreciative, and I remember getting A's on all my art projects the rest of the semester.

Hindsight

I can recall a situation when I was student teaching and couldn't stand my supervising teacher. Ms. Sutter was a proper, well-organized, tight-lipped woman with the face of a lemon and the disposition of a bulldog. Every day she criticized me about my teaching methods, particularly my lack of organizational ability, even in front of the students. When she did, I felt both embarrassed and angry. I wanted to give her a piece of my mind, but I had heard through the grapevine not to express my concerns as she would only become more hostile toward me. By the 6th week, I dreaded having to teach under her critical surveillance. I was about to explode but couldn't. Then I had a chance to get even.

On Wednesday after school, the principal held a staff meeting and I was asked to attend. Just before entering the teacher's lounge, Ms. Sutter stopped by the restroom. When she came out, I noticed her skirt was tucked in the top of her underpants, causing her thighs to be exposed. I didn't say anything, because I knew she would be embarrassed in front of her colleagues, especially since there were several male teachers in the school. When I saw this I just thought, "Perfect, now she knows how it feels to be embarrassed in front of one's colleagues."

Level 4: Hidden but Conscious Revenge

At Level 4 passive-aggressive behavior, the student has hostile feelings toward the teacher and consciously decides to get hidden revenge at a later time. The student thinks, "Okay, you made me do something that I did not want to do, or you treated me without respect, and now you are going to have to pay the price. What will be enjoyable is the fact you will not even have a clue that I did it."

Indiana Joan and the desk of doom

A prim and proper first-year English teacher treated me badly all year long. When handing out spelling tests, she often said, "Well, Wendy, I see you failed again." So I caught two garden snakes on her farm and placed them in the top center drawer of her desk. Without looking, she reached in that drawer for her pen. I couldn't wait for her reaction. Oh boy! I swear her feet did not touch the floor as she fled from that classroom. Whenever I think about it, I still laugh. Most important I never got caught.

Farewell to grades

Looking back at my adolescent years, it's hard to believe I did this. I felt that my 10th-grade science teacher had it in for me and so always assigned me to work with the least knowledgeable student in the class, even though the teacher knew I was very motivated to achieve. I turned in my lab report, which my partner had copied. Mr. Patton confronted me and said, because I allowed my partner to cheat, he was going to drop my grade one letter. This made me furious, but I felt I could do nothing about it. The following week, as we were leaving his class, I noticed that Mr. Patton's grade book was at the edge of his desk. As I walked by it, I gave it a nudge and it dropped off his desk into the wastebasket. I later heard that he was seething with frustration about losing his grade book for all his classes. I remember how much I enjoyed hearing about this catastrophe.

The next example of hidden revenge meets the criteria for inclusion at Level 4 but it is not a serious tactic. The student is angry with the teacher and expresses that anger behind the teacher's back. The goal is not to hurt the teacher but to make fun of the teacher while winning group support.

The tongue

I remember being angry with my English teacher and sticking my tongue out at her as she passed. My classmates saw me do this and laughed. When the teacher turned around, we all looked angelic.

And the finger

My physical education teacher was always pushing us to do more push-ups, chin-ups, and knee bends than I could do. One time I was so ticked by his escalating demands that I gave him the finger sign behind his back. Several of my classmates smiled at me. Without any verbal exchange, I felt vindicated.

Level 5: Self-Depreciation

Level 5 is the most serious level of passive aggression and is beyond the range of a situational reaction. This level of passive-aggressive behavior is a pathological way of expressing anger, most often to parents, but sometimes to teachers as well. The behaviors are so unacceptable or repulsive that the student depreciates himself or herself in the process. While the student may win the power struggle with the parents, the student loses self-esteem, respect from others, and possibly his or her academic future.

Motivated to fail

I have been teaching advanced English in high school for years, but I had never had a student in my class like Alfred. I first thought Alfred was the perfect student. He was intelligent and well read, participated freely in the group discussions, and wrote with unusual fluency and insight for his age. I even felt that Alfred liked me. But when it came to taking my exams, he was sure to receive a low grade. His answers to the test questions were incomplete, fragmented, and sketchy. I wondered if he had test anxiety, but when I observed him taking my exam, he seemed relaxed and comfortable. After receiving a C– mid-semester grade, I asked Alfred to see me during his study hall to discuss my concerns about his low test grades. As we talked about his underachievement, he said that he wasn't interested in grades but only in knowledge. He felt he was learning a lot in my class. I tried to convince him he could have high grades and knowledge, but there was no change in Alfred's test scores for the rest of the semester. I could not or would not fail him because of his class participation, but I was unable to give him an A, which he could have achieved easily.

The following semester, the school psychologist told me she had met with Alfred's parents, and they had decided to transfer him to a private school. The father was particularly upset because he had plans for Alfred to attend Princeton, and he was alarmed that his son would not get in if his grades did not improve. The psychologist was certain that Alfred was in a passive-aggressive battle with his father, and Alfred seemed more motivated to fail and win the battle than to achieve and please his father.

Where are the odor eaters?

Tom was one of the most complicated 11-year-old students I ever taught. He was bright, attractive, and sullen. He rarely smiled, reached out to his peers, or showed any interest in the world around him. I was told that he was physically abused and emotionally disturbed and currently was living with his aunt and uncle. I was told that Tom had a problem, but I did not know much about it. A month later, his problem—as the saying goes—hit the fan.

Tom was not paying attention to my instructions, so I stopped, called his name, and gave him a warning. A few minutes later I noticed he had his head down on his desk, so I interrupted the class and told him he had better pay attention and finish his work or he would have to stay in during recess. My reprimand must have made Tom angry. He gave me a frozen stare and put his head down on the desk again. I told the class to ignore him, because Tom would just sit there until he finished his assignment. Ten minutes later, one of the students said, "What's that smell!? Something stinks in here!" The odor was putrid and reeked throughout the room. The students were gagging, and, as I looked at Tom, I knew. He had defecated in his pants and sat there without any sense of discomfort. When I asked him if he had had an accident, he replied, "Yes," followed by a smirk. The message was clear. Tom got back at me. He seemed to have more pleasure causing me some discomfort than any embarrassment for soiling himself in the classroom. As I talked this incident over with the counselor, she informed me that Tom had a history of soiling himself.

Dressed to kill

I teach at Southgate, a high school in the suburbs of Chicago. Southgate is known for its academic programs and number of merit scholarship winners. The school staff and administration are supportive, and the students are highly motivated to succeed. It is an honor to be on the staff of this school.

When I met my 10th-grade English class for the first time, I was surprised by the appearance of Donna. She wore a black biker's jacket, tattered jeans, a dreadlock hairdo, several body tattoos, and black painted fingernails. She looked like a member of a delinquent gang, and I expected her to say, "What are you looking at?" I was expecting Donna to be vocal and oppositional. Instead, she was quiet and conforming. Her behavior and test scores were inconsistent but acceptable. The girls in my class found her more difficult to accept and reported some of her upsetting comments, such as, "I'm a member of a devil worshiping cult," and "Jews and blacks are destroying our country."

One Monday morning she came to class and refused to do anything. I gave her several options, but nothing seemed to work. Finally, I asked her to leave and see her counselor, which she did without any fuss. Later I heard her mother was coming to a school conference about Donna, and I asked to attend. When Donna's mother arrived and was introduced to the staff, I was shocked by her appearance. She was the absolute opposite of Donna. She looked like she had stepped out of a fashion magazine, or perhaps like the stereotype of the wealthy society woman raising money for the Chicago Symphony.

When Donna entered the room and sat next to her mother, there was no possibility that anyone would guess they were related. The mother started to apologize for Donna's appearance, but stopped and said, "Donna and I have real problems. She seems to do everything she can to upset me. I've asked her a hundred times never to wear these clothes, but she wears them anyway. No wonder she doesn't have any friends or success in school." When Donna was asked to talk about school, she said,

"It's alright. I have no complaints." The conference ended 30 minutes later with little hope that Donna's appearance or behavior would change. The counselor thought that Donna was angry with her mother and was getting back at her passive aggressively by dressing and behaving this way.

Passive-Aggressive Students at Home

Passive aggression exists in many homes and is the silent killer of healthy feelings of comfort, freedom, and intimacy among family members. Passive aggression, like a microscopic mite, floats undetected in the social atmosphere of the home, contaminating the psychological comfort of everyone. No one escapes the infection of passive-aggressive behavior, since everyone develops an allergic reaction to it. This interpretation of family passive aggression challenges the image of the middle-class family viewed as a place of respite from the stresses of life. Instead, we believe many middle-class families are battlegrounds for unexpressed feelings of anger among family members.

The "perfect family" of yesterday, when divorce was uncommon, may be idealized fiction. In reality, the families of yesteryear were as problematic as many of the families of today. For example, Rosenfeld (1997) reported on a conference in Colonial Williamsburg by a panel of 18th-century experts who described a grim picture of family life two centuries ago.

> Eliza Parke Custis was whipped severely after her father removed a cottonseed she had put up her nose. She wrote in her diary, "When he put me down my proud heart swelled with anger. . . . I thought he was unjust and I felt he had degraded me." Thomas Jefferson wrote his eldest daughter, Martha, a student in Annapolis, "If you love me, then strive to be good under every situation and to all living creatures, and to acquire those accomplishments which I have put in your power, and which will go far towards ensuring you the warmest love of your affectionate father. P.S. Keep my letters and read them at times, that you may always have present in your mind those things which will endear you to me."

More fascinating information would be what types of passive-aggressive behaviors Eliza Custis and Martha Jefferson no doubt expressed toward their famous fathers.

REASONS FOR PASSIVE-AGGRESSIVE BEHAVIOR AT HOME

In Chapter 2, we described the various reasons why passive aggression exists. The following are the most common reasons for passive-aggressive behavior to occur in families:

1. **Fear of retaliation** from an authoritarian, abusive, alcoholic, or perfectionistic parent.

2. **Parental suppression of anger** due to excessive standards of goodness, social approval, and guilt. The following statements reflect this parental behavior:

- "Shame on you for talking to me that way."

- "Don't you know it's a sin to be angry at your parents?"

- "Until you show me the respect I deserve by apologizing, you will stay in your room!"

- "You just wait! You'll be sorry you acted that way because good girls don't use that language."

- "Show me you are not angry at me anymore. Come give me a hug and a kiss."

3. **The behavior of adolescents striving for independence,** a developmental phase.

4. **The problem of intimacy between husband and wife.** This problem results when one partner believes the other partner is available to satisfy all of his or her emotional needs. This irrational belief creates an expectation that is impossible to achieve in a marriage or social situation. It isolates the couple from their friends and family and creates unexpressed feelings of anger as the partners frustrate and disappoint each other. Unable to express their feelings, they falsely tolerate each other's angry attitudes and behaviors. They appear powerless to talk about the irritating behaviors they experience because any discussion of a spouse's behavior might upset the other person. More important, they are unlikely to talk about their own wants and emotional needs. The compromise is to be polite to each other and to express their anger in passive-aggressive ways. It is the civilized middle-class way of avoiding intimacy. Actually, passive-aggressive parents are often thought of as pleasant parents who hide their anger. One student wrote,

> My parents never fought or expressed an angry word to each other as long as I can remember. But I knew when they were angry with each other, and I felt sad when they would withdraw and not speak. I remember asking them what was wrong; but they *always* would answer, politely, "Everything is fine."

5. **The problem of failed expectations of students with a disability.**

As discussed in Chapter 4, the expression of passive-aggressive anger occurs in families at all five levels of intensity, ranging from common to pathological acts. The most common way of expressing passive-aggressive behavior is at the level of temporary compliance.

Level 1: Temporary Compliance

At Level 1, the child agrees to comply with the parent's request but then does not do it. Procrastination, postponement, stalling, and forgetting to do something are typical examples of this level of passive-aggressive behavior. When confronted, the child will provide endless excuses to justify the procrastination or unwillingness to carry out the request. Sometimes these excuses are simply normal expressions of individuals who are involved in other interests, are tired, or perceive the request as unnecessary. Only when the response derives from personal anger is the behavior really passive aggressive. A child at this level of passive aggression is motivated to get back at someone while justifying his or her own behavior. The following are either normal responses or passive-aggressive responses depending on the underlying motivation:

MOTHER:	Come in the house now.
BILLY:	I'm coming, Mother. (Does not come in.)
DAD:	Did you turn the hose off?
MARY:	I will but I had to go to the bathroom.
GRANDMOTHER:	Will you come and help me now?
TODD:	Sure, right after this TV show is over.
DAD:	Did you answer the phone?
NANCY:	I didn't hear it.
MOM:	Are you ready for school?
BETHANY:	My stomach hurts, and I can't find my books.
BROTHER:	Did you bring my book back from school?
SISTER:	I gave it to Tom. I didn't know you wanted it back.

We are all familiar with these excuses. They are heard in most families. The important considerations are whether the behavior derives from personal anger and whether the behavior is intended to hurt or frustrate the adult or is designed to maintain the person's current activity.

Cinderella has a ball

My stepmother and stepsister were thorns in my side throughout my high school years. One thorn in *their* side was my academic success. My stepmother got upset when she saw my report cards and yelled at her daughter that she should study like me. Each night I sat at the kitchen table and studied, whether or not I really had homework. Stepmother often remarked how hard I studied. My stepsister and I were in the same mathematics class, but I got A's, and she was failing. Many times she'd ask me for my math homework, and I said, "Sure, here you are," with a nice, big smile. I knew that she would end up failing the course anyway, because I never showed her how to do the math. She just copied it. (Smile.)

Level 2: Intentional Inefficiency

This level of passive-aggressive behavior occurs when a student expresses anger toward an adult by completing the request, but in a way that will upset the adult, as in the following example:

MOTHER: Every time I ask you to do something for me, you mess it up!

ADOLESCENT: Yes, and you keep on asking me.

For whom do the wedding bells toll?

This is probably the first of many tales to tell about the source of my stress, my mother-in-law. Joni and I had just become engaged. Fantastic! Everything was great until I learned that my future in-laws were planning an engagement party extravaganza with rented hall, catered food, band, the whole bit. Okay, I guess I could live through it. It should be a fun party, anyway.

As time went on, I began feeling that the party was getting out of hand. Every time I made a suggestion about the music or some other component my idea was politely dismissed as inappropriate. After several weeks, I became all too aware of exactly who was financing this thing and who was deciding on all arrangements. At some point, I agreed to show up for the party *but* that would be the total extent of my participation.

One week before the extravaganza, Joni's mother began dropping hints: "You look so nice without a beard." "Don't you think a trim would make your hair look neater?" "Don't come right away; maybe you and Joni should arrive later, after the guests." That was it! She was making too many suggestions, and I felt she was inhibiting my personal freedom. She even went so far as to buy me a suit for the occasion and suggested I might want to select a shirt and tie.

The Christmas before, Joni had made me a pendant comprised of parts from several junked clocks. I decided to wear that to the party. I felt it was totally appropriate and quite a handsome piece. When my future mother-in-law heard about my plans, she broke down into sobs of distress, crying uncontrollably. It did my heart good! But after a moment, the impossible happened! I actually felt sorry for her!

I wore a tie, but not the suit, arrived in time to greet the guests, and had a good time. But for that brief moment in time, *revenge was sweet!*

Play it again, Sam

My mother said it was time to practice for my piano lesson, but there was a baseball game going down the block. What kid likes to stay in and practice scales when he could be sliding into home plate? I said, "Okay," and started to play off-key and very loudly. If she was going to make me practice, I was going to irritate the heck out of her. Mother yelled, "Sammy, you know how to play better than that." I shot back, "Look, I'm doing what you asked. You have no right to get angry with me." After about 5 minutes, my mom said I could go outside and then practice the piano after supper. I learned this was a successful way of getting my way while also getting back at my mom.

Getting to the grass roots of the problem

Our adolescent son, Ralph, has the responsibility of cutting the lawn on our weekend property every Saturday. This particular Saturday, he said,

"Dad there is a soccer game at school. Can I have a break, and I'll cut the lawn later in the afternoon?" I felt this was an acceptable alternative, so I agreed. Unfortunately, it rained all afternoon, so Ralph couldn't cut the lawn. The following weekend, the grass was quite high, and being a typical father, I said to him, "Ralph, when you cut the grass today with the tractor, I want you to do a good job. I don't want you to put the tractor into high gear and cut the grass at 20 miles an hour. Since you didn't cut the grass last week and it's hot today, I want you to take your time. In fact, you may have to cut it twice to do a good job."

Clearly, he was disgusted with me and my comments. He knew how to cut the lawn and he didn't need to have his dad treat him like a child. He said, "You want a good job. All right, I'll give you a good job." Off he goes and is on the tractor for about 2 hours. When he comes into the house he is sweaty and says, "Dad, you will be happy. I cut the grass just the way you wanted, nice and neat and low." I walked outdoors and saw about one and a half acres of dirt. I couldn't see one blade of grass. He set the lawnmower blade so low that the grass was cut to its roots. He did what I asked him to do, but in a way that made me furious.

The joylessness of cooking

I enjoy cooking and want to share this skill with my 13-year-old daughter who is in special education. One Sunday afternoon, I decided I would teach her how to make a bundt cake, although she didn't seem interested in this culinary adventure. I showed her how to take eggs and crack them in the bowl and to add the milk, flour, and sugar. Of course, Stefi wanted to listen to the radio while we were baking. She cracked five eggs correctly but the sixth egg missed the bowl, hit the counter, and slid down to the floor. We stopped and cleaned it up. After all, accidents do occur. She started to beat the batter by putting the bowl on her hip and stirring while dancing to the sound of the music. Inevitably, the batter started running down her leg until I couldn't stand it anymore. Finally I exclaimed, "That's it Stefi, get out of the kitchen, you're destroying everything!" As Stefi went out the door, she stated, "Geez, Mom, how am I ever going to learn to make a bundt cake if you don't teach me?"

Level 3: Letting a Problem Escalate

At times, the passive-aggressive person can worsen a situation by doing nothing when he or she knows that by doing something the situation could be improved. The following examples demonstrate that a person who is passive-aggressive may get pleasure out of a family member's mistake or unnecessary mishap.

Driving Mr. Daisy crazy

I have been in therapy for the past 2 years to work out a better marital relationship with my husband. Sometimes I wonder why we ever got married in the first place, since we are such different personality types and enjoy such opposite lifestyles. Jerry is a powerful, successful, and superorganized attorney. He believes the early bird gets the worm; he gets up each morning at 5:00 A.M. Before going to bed at 9:30 P.M., he programs the coffee maker so his coffee will be hot and ready at 5:00. Following coffee, he has a large glass of orange juice and a bowl of Total. He exercises for the next 30 minutes using his weights and treadmill. Then he showers, shaves and dresses, and is off to work by 6:30. Intermittently, I wonder if he is a robot. What I like to do is to go to bed after "The Tonight Show" and get up at 8:30 to catch the last 30 minutes of "The Today Show."

I consider myself a relaxed, laid-back, easygoing woman, who doesn't like to race through life. I enjoy reading the newspaper in the morning, talking to my friends, and participating in various community activities. Our marriage seems to operate on the unexpressed agreement of "I won't bother you, if you don't bother me!" This arrangement works out most of the time, except when we go on one of our weeklong car trips to a national monument or park. I dread these trips and find them anything but pleasant. Jerry, of course, organizes these trips down to the minute. His plan is to have the car packed, gassed, and ready to go the night before we leave. We are to get up at 5:30 A.M. and leave at 6:00 A.M. with a thermos of coffee in hand. His goal is to drive for 2 hours and then stop for breakfast for 40 minutes. Then we are to drive for 3 1/2 more hours and check in to a Holiday Inn by 1:00 P.M. We are to unpack, have lunch, take a swim, and do other relaxing activities.

Last August I had an opportunity to assert myself during one of these trips. Jerry had planned to drive us to the Blue Ridge Mountains of West Virginia. We left at 6:00 A.M. on schedule and drove West on U.S. 70. In 1 hour we would turn South on U.S. 81. Jerry was driving faster than the speed limit although it was a foggy and damp day. His driving was beginning to irritate me, but I bit my lip. Then I noticed a highway sign flash by: "U.S. 81, 1 mile." I realized Jerry didn't see it, since he was not slowing down. I decided not to say anything to him until we passed the exit. Two miles later, I said, "Darling, have you changed your mind about turning on U.S. 81?" He looked surprised and said, "Do you mean we missed it?" I nodded and he shouted, "Why didn't you tell me?" "Darling," I replied sweetly, "You are so well organized I never thought for a moment you had made a mistake. I just thought you had decided on a different route." Jerry was beside himself and had to drive another 8 miles before finding the next exit to turn around. His mistake meant his schedule was off by 20 minutes, but I had a day's worth of satisfaction.

Sisters are a girl's worst friend

It was Friday evening, and it looked like I'd be sitting home watching TV with my younger brothers. My 19-year-old sister, Suzanne, was getting ready for her date. It had been a week since we'd argued over who *really* owned the stockings hanging in the bathroom, and she was still giving me "the silent treatment." Suzanne came downstairs to get some toothpaste and passed me in the hall, nearly knocking me over. She smiled ever so sweetly and said, "Oh, I'm sorry! I didn't see you coming!"

I went into the living room to turn on the TV, trying to resign myself to the situation. Great! The TV volume was too loud, and as I was pushing every button on the remote, I barely heard the telephone ringing. This, I thought, could be my chance to go out! I realized the phone had been answered upstairs. I ran to it and lifted the receiver, only to hear a male voice say, "Okay, thank you." Click. Oh no! I ran upstairs and Suzanne said, "Oh, I thought you went out for the evening. That call was for you." And then, with that sweet tone of voice, she added, "Oh, I'm so sorry."

"Gee, honey, I'm sorry"

I never thought I was a passive-aggressive person until I attended your seminar. The diagnostic categories were so clear I had no difficulty identifying myself. I did have a problem admitting I felt some joy and satisfaction when I got back at some frustrating person. The one example I will always remember happened when I was angry with my wife for nagging me. I deliberately got back at her. At the time I felt vindicated, but later I felt guilty.

I have been married to Cynthia for 15 years and she has several behaviors that irritate me. The one that is most upsetting is her obsession to be at work on time regardless of the driving conditions. Let me explain.

We both work in downtown Chicago so we drive together, or more precisely I need to drive her to her office by 8:30 A.M. Since it is a 45-minute commute, we leave our condo no later than 7:30. This particular Thursday, I had a difficult night sleeping. I was up three times so when the alarm went off at 6:30, I was not in a good or active mood. Cynthia, of course, woke up in high gear and was finished dressing before I started my shower. Then she started in on me.

"Robert, do you realize you have only 25 minutes before we leave?" "Robert, you need to hurry up." "Robert, you know I have an important meeting this morning so I can't be late." "Robert, I don't think you will have time for breakfast." "Robert, I am going to be mad if you make me late." "Robert, why do you do this to me? Why can't you get organized in the morning?!"

By this time, I was boiling but I didn't say anything.

We left at 7:50 and before I drove out of the garage, she said, "I know I am going to be late and it is all your fault! I don't know why I even drive with you in the morning!"

I didn't reply but I thought her last angry comment seemed like a good idea to me. We didn't speak to each other the remainder of the trip, but I remember I deliberately drove in the slowest lane and stopped at every red light possible.

We arrived at 8:30. She jumped out of the car, sarcastically said, "Thanks for the ride," and slammed the door. I started to drive away when I noticed she had left her briefcase with all the documents she needed for her meeting on the back seat. I quickly accelerated and smiled, "Okay, Cynthia, now it's your turn." I even had the pleasant

NOTES

thought that her compulsive boss might yell at her and tell her she needed to get better organized in the morning.

When I arrived at work I called her and said in a sympathetic tone, "Cynthia, I just discovered your briefcase on the back seat of the car and called you immediately." Cynthia said she realized she left it the moment she entered the building but when she ran back to the curb I was gone. I told her I was sorry I didn't see it sooner. She asked in a subdued tone if I could possibly bring it over to her work. I said I wish I could but I had a scheduled appointment *all morning*. She thanked me for the call and said she would pick it up during her lunch hour. I knew she was close to tears, but when she hung up, I remember saying to myself, "Touché!"

Level 4: Hidden but Conscious Revenge

A Level 4 passive-aggressive act is a hateful, deliberate deed. The person has hateful feelings toward a sibling or parent and decides to get back at a later time in a conscious act of hostility and revenge.

Elixir of hate

I never told anyone about what I did to my sister, Terry, about 15 years ago. Perhaps writing about this incident will relieve some of the guilt I still feel when I think about it. Terry is 2 years older than I and had it all. She was beautiful, had a great figure, did well in school, had lots of friends, and even got along with our parents. I thought she was nice to everyone but me. One fall day, she told me Derek was taking her to a picnic at one of our local parks in Wisconsin. I thought Derek was gorgeous, and I was envious. Terry then giggled and said, "Too bad you don't have a date, because this is going to be a great party." With that comment I decided I was going to get back at her. I wondered how I could do it without her finding out. Finally, I came up with an ingenious idea. Terry would protect her beautiful skin by putting on mosquito repellent before she left. I went to the bathroom and found the bottle of repellent. I emptied half of it and filled it up with baby-oil. I shook it and left it for Terry to find. Before she left, she dabbed it on her hands and face. When she returned, she was peppered with mosquito bites. She was crying and said, "I don't know what happened. It seemed like hundreds of bugs were always around me." I told her how sorry I was this had happened to her, while in my heart, I knew it was because of my lotion potion.

The proof was in the stuffing

As the middle child in a family with a sister 2 years older and a brother 1 year younger, I found that I could not act out my anger directly. My sister was both physically and verbally superior to me, and my brother, though younger, was always bigger and stronger. When I was about 9, I discovered that I could get back at them in an indirect way, which I can now see as passive-aggressive behavior. I would take some object that they used daily, such as a brush, which they normally kept in a certain place. They would go to use it, and it would have just disappeared. I would hear them mumbling to themselves, then ask my mother if she had seen it. When they asked me, I'd tell them I had no idea where they had put it. I didn't steal the objects; rather, I would hide them. I enjoyed knowing I could cause them distress without accepting responsibility for it. I had forgotten how often I had used this technique until I went to college and found a pair of my sister's gloves that I had stuffed in a hole in a stuffed animal.

Level 5: Self-Depreciation

As stated earlier, self-depreciation is the most serious level of passive aggression and represents a pathological expression of anger in most cases. The person is so angry that he or she gets hurt in the process of retaliation, and self-abuse becomes a consequence of the power struggle. Moreover, the person's behaviors are so unacceptable that he or she forfeits self-esteem and the respect of his or her family members.

Less for Lester

I was a plump teen in a slim family. I stopped eating normally at about age 15. Rather rapidly I lost so much weight that my parents insisted on therapy, which culminated in my hospitalization for anorexia nervosa. The doctors helped me begin to eat nutrients enough to maintain a thin but not skeletal appearance. When I met Les, my husband, I weighed about 100 pounds and looked fine though fragile. My husband wanted me to put "more meat on my bones" and sometimes became annoyed when he was eating steak and pasta and I, my salad.

Recently the issue of my gaining 10 pounds became the central topic for continued discussion with Lester. He constantly bugged me to gain the extra weight. When he decided to go visit his parents by himself for a week, I was verbally supportive of his independent activity and understanding of his need for a meeting with his aging folks. Although he questioned me about my feelings, I assured him that I really wanted him to enjoy this time alone with his family. Upon his return, however, he found me awaiting his arrival weighing 5 pounds less. Instead of dealing with my true feelings related to his private meeting and feelings of exclusion, I acted out in a way that I knew would annoy him. I consider my weight loss a passive-aggressive act.

Counter–Passive Aggression

In the previous chapters, the passive-aggressive student was the focus. The etiology of passive aggression, the dynamics of hidden anger, and the various ways a passive-aggressive student successfully frustrates others at school and home were discussed. This chapter focuses on a neglected but significant dynamic of passive aggression, the *target* of the passive-aggressive student—that is, the teacher or parent who inadvertently reinforces the student's passive-aggressive behavior. Once this circular pattern of passive-aggressive behavior and counter–passive-aggressive behavior occurs, the adult has no hope for an enjoyable or comfortable relationship with the student. The choice for the adult is either to continue to relate to the student on an emotional roller coaster of confusion, anger, and guilt, or to learn to understand and control the counter–passive-aggressive behavior.

THE CONCEPT OF COUNTER–PASSIVE AGGRESSION

The concept of counter–passive aggression represents a new insight into the dynamics of the passive-aggressive student. The concept of counter–passive aggression has been the missing piece of the psychological puzzle in understanding passive aggression. It explains why reasonable and rational teachers and parents react to a passive-aggressive student in counter–passive-aggressive ways.

To reinforce this concept, consider the relationship between a movie director and her lead actor. The movie director (the passive-aggressive person) tells the actor (the non–passive-aggressive person) that he needs to develop more authenticity in his character. The director demonstrates the scene and says, "Now, I want you to mirror my emotions and behavior. I want you to act in this scene exactly like I do. This will not be easy, because you have to give up your normal way of relating to others in order to take on my persona."

This description is exactly what happens when a student who is passive aggressive relates to an adult. Over time, the adult ends up behaving like the student, in ways that are not characteristic of the adult's personality. Many times the adult is shocked and appalled to be behaving counter–passive aggressively and is dismayed to have acted in such a childish and nonprofessional way.

The concept of counter–passive aggression is expressed as follows:

In a stressful situation, the student who is passive aggressive will create underlying feelings of anger in the adult and if the adult is unaware of this process and acts on his or her current feelings of anger, the adult will mirror the student's passive-aggressive behavior. As a result, the adult will behave in counter–passive-aggressive ways.

The following examples illustrate how adults who are not typically passive aggressive react to passive-aggressive students by mirroring counter–passive-aggressive behaviors. In all of these examples, the adult never confronts the passive-aggressive student about his or her underlying anger. Instead, the adult reacts by behaving in counter–passive-aggressive ways.

EXAMPLES OF COUNTER–PASSIVE AGGRESSION

In addition to the five levels of passive-aggressive behavior, we have documented four types of counter–passive-aggressive behavior by adults.

Type 1: Counter–Temporary Compliance

Type 1 is a perfect mirror of Level I called temporary compliance. Like the student's behavior, the adult gets back by procrastinating and feigning temporary blindness, deafness, or brain damage.

Later, my love

There are a number of passive-aggressive students in my class whom I find irritating. I didn't realize how they were getting me to reflect their behavior. As I thought about it, I came up with the following examples. Steven would raise his hand, and I would say, "I'll be there in a minute," but I'd never return. Cathy would ask me to bring in the science journal I mentioned. I would reply, "I forgot. I'm sorry. I'll bring it tomorrow." But I didn't.

Under my skin

Carl is my classroom aide. When I ask him to do anything, he frequently mumbles so I have to ask him again to repeat what he said. I have observed that he speaks clearly to other staff. Recently, when he has asked me for something like the time of a meeting, I have mumbled to him. Then Carl asks, "What did you say?" It dawned on me that I have been acting just like Carl.

Holding on

My 13-year-old daughter usually responds to any request with the comment, "Hold o-o-o-n." Over time it began to upset me. Last week, she was in a rush to get to a skating party and I was the driver. So I calmly said, "Hold o-o-o-n," and took my sweet time getting ready to go.

Type 2: Counter–Intentional Inefficiency

Type 2 also mirrors the student's behavior of intentional inefficiency. The adult gets back at the student's passive-aggressive behavior by not maintaining customary standards of teaching.

How she won the battle but lost the war

My job is to meet with principals who request special transportation for their students. When I arrived at one school, the secretary told me to go right in. When I entered, the principal was sitting at her desk. I said, "Hello." She didn't look up or reply, but she continued to look through a directory while she kept me standing. After 2 minutes, she said, "What can I do for you?" I wanted to say, "Lady, you can show me some good manners," but I didn't. I explained why I was there and asked her to complete a form justifying her request for class trips.

As she filled out the form, I was still brooding about how rudely she treated me. When she handed me the forms, I looked at them, thanked her, and smiled. I noticed she had not answered one of the important questions on the form and I knew her request would be rejected. She would have to reapply and begin at the bottom of the list of requests. I made it clear to my supervisor that the problem was her mistake and not mine.

Several days later, I thought about this situation and I was not happy with the way I handled it. This was not typical of me. I let my feelings get the best of me, but at the time it felt like the right thing to do.

Type 3: Intentional Overefficiency

This category of counter–passive aggression is the opposite of intentional inefficiency. Teachers and parents have authority and responsibility for carrying out certain policies, rules, and regulations in school and at home. At times, parents and teachers can rely on policies, rules, and regulations in an unprofessional way. They can express their anger toward a passive-aggressive student by hiding behind these policies, rules, and regulations. They can use them in counter–passive-aggressive ways that allow them to punish and get back at the student without feeling guilty. Teachers are in an ideal position to become counter–passive aggressive with their students, since they have the power to call on students, to question students, and to evaluate their work and behavior. In addition, they have the authority to report student problems to the principal or the student's parents. They can justify their behavior by saying, "I was only doing my job."

Two can play this game

Clarisse, a student with a learning disability who is in my class, has been annoying me for weeks. Last week during social studies, I asked the class the question, "Who can tell me the complete name of the First Lady?" Clarisse knew the answer and was the first student to raise her hand. I looked at her but called on Don. Clarisse looked disappointed that I didn't call on her. If someone had observed this interaction and asked me why I didn't call on Clarisse, I would say, "I have 30 students in my class, and I can't always call on her." Later I asked a difficult question, "Who can tell me the name of the bank the First Lady worked for? It was mentioned in your reading assignment last night." It was unlikely Clarisse knew the answer, so I called on her. She began to mumble, stutter, hem-and-haw. I said politely, "Clarisse, we want you to be part of this class. But you're really going to have to study more. So please, please read your assignments." While Clarisse looked embarrassed, I was enjoying the situation and thinking, "This time it was my turn."

Higher Standards, Lower Grades

One of the most effective ways a teacher can get back at a passive-aggressive student is to evaluate his or her work critically. For example, when the student turns in an assignment, the teacher can get out the red pencil and critique it by writing "it's too long," "it's too short," "too fragmented," "too many dangling participles," "incorrect margins," "the i's aren't dotted," "the t's aren't crossed," "Grade D."

If the parents confront the teacher by saying their son seems to get an unusual number of red marks on his papers, the teacher can quietly hide behind her professional role and say, "Are you criticizing me because I have high standards and took the extra time to give your son realistic feedback? I'm appalled, because most parents complain that teachers don't do enough for their children." These comments create a perfect Catch-22 situation for the parents, while protecting the teacher from further criticism for the student's low grade.

Searching for the Flaw

I observed this example of a teacher's counter–passive-aggressive behavior during a math lesson. The teacher asked two students to go to the blackboard and answer different problems. Jennifer was given the fraction 8/64 and asked to reduce it to its lowest common denominator. Jennifer wrote 1/8 and was praised for her answer. Steve, a passive-aggressive student, was given the fraction 3/285 and asked to reduce it to its lowest common denominator. Steve thought about it and wrote 1/95.

The teacher looked at Steve and asked, "Are you sure?" Steve looked quizzical and said, "Yes, 1/95." The teacher continued by saying, "Are you absolutely sure?" By now Steve was confused and replied, "Well, 1/96?" The teacher said, "Well, what is it? Is it 1/96 or 1/95?" Steve said he thought it was 1/95. She retorted, "Don't tell me what you think. Tell me what you know. Is it 1/95 or 1/96?" Steve was now in a state of anxiety and said, "It's 1/95." The teacher said, "Certainly, it's 1/95 but look how you wrote your 5!" She walked over to the blackboard, erased his 5 and made a perfect 5. She said, "You need to write your letters more clearly or someday it will get you into trouble." The teacher was successful in frustrating the student by becoming counter–passive aggressive even though Steve had the correct answer.

Type 4: Letting a Problem Escalate, Counter-Escalation

Counter-escalation is a common response by parents who have passive-aggressive children, particularly if they have a disability. Parents can become so overwhelmed by the constant barrage of passive-aggressive behaviors that they, at times, will allow the child's behavior to escalate. A distinction needs to be made between parents who let the behavior escalate so that the child learns from his or her inappropriate behavior and those parents who enjoy their child's subsequent plight. When a parent goes through the pain and decides to let the child experience the logical consequences of the inappropriate behavior, the child hopefully will learn from the experience. This is an appropriate child-rearing technique. However, if the parent is angry with the child's passive-aggressive behavior and enjoys the child's dilemma, the child will not learn anything productive about his or her own behavior from the experience. The child will perceive it as an act of punishment by the parents and not a natural function of his or her behavior.

Morning madness

It's 6:30 A.M. . . . Ugh! I stumble out of bed to awaken my two boys to get ready for school at 7:30. Lewis, who is 8 years old, immediately gets up and goes to the bathroom to brush his teeth, thus commencing his organized pattern of preparing for school. "How easy Lewis is," I mumble as I approach to awaken James, who is a chronological 10-year-old but a 3-year-old regarding his ability to get it together in the morning. His response to my wake-up call is "I'm tired. I still want to sleep." Unhappy at what appears to be the beginning of yet another unpleasant morning ritual, I leave the room, thinking he can stay in bed even though he explicitly stated last night it was important for him to get up on time due to unfinished homework and unwashed hair.

7:15 A.M. Lewis is finishing his breakfast as James, in jeans and shirt but no shoes or socks, enters the kitchen and sits down to eat. While he is eating breakfast, I comment on how little time James has to finish his homework. James starts to panic, realizing that finishing breakfast, finding his shoes, doing his homework, and washing his hair are impossible to accomplish in 15 minutes.

7:30 A.M. James, after spending a very harried 15 minutes, is ready to leave. As he is going out the front door, I suggest he look at himself in the mirror. He sees that he has not even brushed his hair, let alone washed it. Now he begins to fall apart. "How can I go to school looking like this? Where is a brush?" he asks me. I respond, "Wherever you left it." "Mom, please help me," he pleads. As I go to find the brush, I ask him, "Why can't you ever get ready in time?"

7:33 A.M. James frantically brushes his hair. As he leaves in an anxious state, I tell him, "Have a nice day, Honey," knowing that he will have to run two blocks to catch the bus.

Time to take your turn

I teach in a small elementary school with 16 staff members. Rarely do we have time for a civilized lunchtime. We usually bring a brown bag lunch or some dish to warm in the microwave. No one ever seemed to be in charge of the teachers' room. I like my room to be neat and clean, but this room was always a mess by the end of each day.

Three months ago I suggested we keep a daily cleanup list and take turns being responsible for tidying the area at lunch and at the end of the school day. This seemed to work well for everyone but Mary Anne, who always had an excuse for not tidying up on her day. By the third time she neglected her responsibility, I was really ticked. The next day I opened the fridge and saw a little bag marked "M.A." Impulsively, I grabbed her bag, looked around, threw it in the trash can, covered it with other garbage, and left hastily. When she began asking about her lunch, I smiled my secret smile and said nothing. I know this was not the right thing to do. I felt guilty but I also told myself she deserved it!

A Word of Warning Regarding the Concept of Counter–Passive Aggression

The concept of counter–passive aggression is critical to understanding the psychology of passive aggression. After one of our seminars, a teacher came up to us and said, "I want you to know how much I enjoyed the concept of staff counter–passive-aggressive behavior. I thought your examples were excellent ways of getting back at students for passive-aggressive behavior. I wondered if you had any other examples I could use in my classroom."

We were stunned and surprised by his comment and said, "I'm afraid we didn't make ourselves clear. We are *not* advocating the use of counter–passive-aggressive behaviors with students. We are trying to do just the opposite. We believe counter–passive-aggressive techniques *are not* to be used in the classroom or at home. We were merely trying to make teachers aware of them, so they won't unknowingly use them." He looked chagrined, said, "Oh," and walked away. After this incident, we made a decision to clarify the inappropriate use of counter–passive-aggressive behavior by adults. This incident also illustrates that nothing in life is so simple or so concrete that it cannot be misinterpreted by someone.

The New Psychology

his chapter brings together all the concepts from the previous chapters into a mosaic, creating a picture of our new psychology of passive aggression. For years, researchers have studied how a teacher's negative behavior can alter and shape students' behavior. What often is forgotten is how the students' negative behavior can alter and shape teachers' behavior. This concept is expressed by the following psychological principle:

▶ A student in stress can create in others his or her feelings, and if the others are unaware of this psychological process, they will mirror the student's inappropriate behavior.

Psychologically, this statement means that an aggressive student can create counteraggressive behavior in others, a depressed student can create counterdepression in others, an indecisive person can create ambivalence in others, and a passive-aggressive student can create counter–passive aggression in others. These reactions often are atypical of the adult's personality. The Conflict Cycle Paradigm was developed by N. Long (1996) to describe this circular and escalating behavior between a passive-aggressive student and a teacher or parent.

OVERVIEW OF THE CONFLICT CYCLE PARADIGM

The Conflict Cycle Paradigm is a conceptual model that explains the escalating interactions between a troubled person and a nontroubled person. This model, presented in Figure 8.1, consists of five sequential circular stages:

▶ **Stage 1.** The troubled person's self-concept.

▶ **Stage 2.** A stressful incident for the troubled person.

▶ **Stage 3.** The feelings of the troubled person.

▶ **Stage 4.** The behavior of the troubled person.

▶ **Stage 5.** The negative reaction by others, which in turn creates more psychological stress, more intense feelings, more insightful behaviors, and more rejecting and primitive reactions, until the initial manageable conflict escalates into a no-win power struggle.

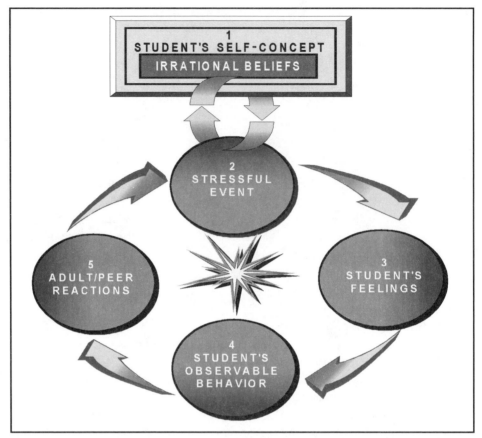

FIGURE 8.1. The Conflict Cycle. *Note.* From "The Conflict Cycle Paradigm on How Troubled Students Get Teachers Out of Control" (p. 245), by N. Long, in *Conflict in the Classroom,* by N. J. Long and W. C. Morse (Eds.), 1996, Austin, TX: PRO-ED. Copyright 1996 by PRO-ED. Reprinted with permission.

The following is the predictable sequence that occurs in the Conflict Cycle Paradigm:

1. An incident occurs (i.e., frustration, failure, disappointment) that is processed by the student's self-concept. This process may ACTIVATE the student's irrational beliefs (i.e., "Nothing good ever happens to me!" "Adults are always demanding!"), which define the incident as stressful for him or her.

2. The student's negative thoughts and not the incident TRIGGER his or her feelings.

3. The student's intense feelings DRIVE his or her inappropriate behaviors.

4. The student's inappropriate behaviors (yelling, threatening, sarcasm, refusing to speak, etc.) INCITE adults.

5. Teachers not only pick up on the student's feelings, but also frequently MIRROR the identical behaviors (yelling back, threatening, sarcasm, refusing to speak, etc.).

6. These negative adult REACTIONS escalate the troubled student's level of stress, fueling the conflict into a self-defeating power struggle.

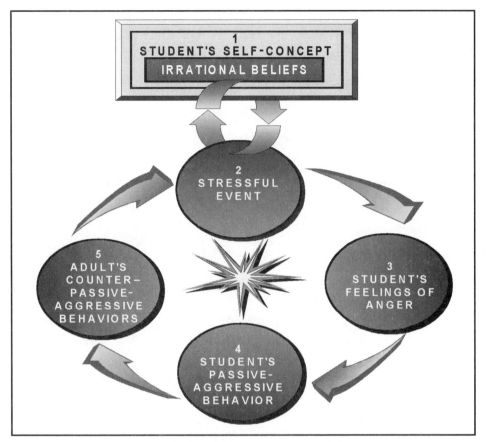

FIGURE 8.2. The Passive-Aggressive Conflict Cycle. *Note.* Adapted from "The Conflict Cycle Paradigm on How Troubled Students Get Teachers Out of Control" (pp. 244–264), by N. Long, in *Conflict in the Classroom*, by N. J. Long and W. C. Morse (Eds.), 1996, Austin, TX: PRO-ED. Copyright 1996 by PRO-ED. Adapted with permission.

THE CONFLICT CYCLE PARADIGM FOR PASSIVE-AGGRESSIVE STUDENTS

When the Conflict Cycle Paradigm is applied to passive-aggressive students, an additional and rewarding insight occurs. Like the gestalt principle that states "the whole is greater than the sum of its parts," our psychology of passive aggression becomes more understandable and comprehensive than the knowledge of the individual characteristics of the passive-aggressive student. The Passive-Aggressive Conflict Cycle (see Figure 8.2) becomes the paradigm for explaining the dynamics of passive aggression.

▶ Stage 1: The Self-Concept of the Passive-Aggressive Student

Stage 1 represents the student's developmental life history and how the student developed a passive-aggressive personality. The student's self-concept has two interdependent functions: (1) the development of beliefs about himself or herself and (2) the development of beliefs about how others in his world will treat him or her. For example, we have found that students who are passive aggressive believe that the direct expression of anger is both dangerous and destructive. Their psychological solution to this problem is to conceal their anger behind a facade of irritating passive-aggressive behaviors. Like the tip of an iceberg, the real size and power of their anger is out of sight to others. For the passive-aggressive student, the expression of anger is not a misdemeanor but a felony.

The following statements were expressed by passive-aggressive students who told us how they feel about anger and aggressive behavior:

- "Angry feelings are upsetting. When people become angry, they yell and scream, and they scare me."

- "When people get angry, terrible things can happen, so there is no telling what I would do if I ever got angry and got out of control."

- "I don't let people know when I'm angry. If they knew what I was thinking, they would hate me and maybe want to kill me."

- "Thinking about anger is wrong, but at times it does excite me."

- "When I'm treated unfairly by others, I'm smart enough to know how to get back at them so they will suffer like they made me suffer."

- "Most teachers and adults are fools. When I'm angry, I can pretend not to hear them."

- "I have to be careful not to let my anger out. It is a demon I have to guard all the time."

These personal statements about anger and aggression highlight the intensity of these students' internalized beliefs. Once a passive-aggressive way of life is internalized, the student will reinforce his or her beliefs by responding to new and demanding interpersonal relationships in passive-aggressive ways. In addition, there are secondary rewards for having a passive-aggressive personality. Although a passive-aggressive personality is defined as a psychological disorder, passive-aggressive behavior serves as a form of personal adjustment and protects the student from the painful feelings of anxiety and helplessness. Passive-aggressive personality is useful because it brings order to an unstable world by making life predictable and manageable. A passive-aggressive personality allows a student to know in advance what will happen in any new relationship while taking away any responsibility for the student's behavior by blaming others for his or her troubles. The student with passive-aggressive personality rarely sees himself or herself as the source of the problem. Moreover, the student is proud of his or her ability to control anger and for not acting so immaturely and emotionally. Simultaneously, the student feels smart and clever for the various ways he or she can get back at others indirectly and without their knowledge. This awareness often gives the student an emotional high and a feeling of power and pleasure for manipulating others so easily.

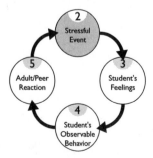

▶ Stage 2: The Student's Stressful Incident

Ninety percent of stressful incidents are determined by how a person learned to think about them and not by the reality of the situation. The image of a glass of water that is half full or half empty is an example of this statement. It is how an individual thinks about the presenting incident that determines whether or not it is to be perceived as stressful. For example, when a passive-aggressive person is asked or told to do a specific task, such as helping with a family chore, rewriting a school assignment, sharing equipment, or attending a weekend work conference, the task may activate her irrational beliefs:

- "I always have to do what they want."

- "I never get to do what I want."

- "They are trying to control me again."

- "They are putting too much pressure on me."

- "These demands are stupid."

Once a connection is made between the presenting incident and the student's irrational beliefs, the student will perceive the presenting incident as stressful.

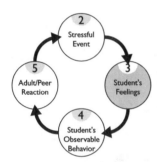

▶ Stage 3: The Student's Feelings

David Burns (1999), a cognitive therapist, writes, "You feel the way you think" (p. 28). The source of feelings begins in the thoughts and not with the presenting incident. It is how a person thinks about an external event, and not the event itself that *triggers* the feelings. Positive thoughts about an event (e.g., "I can handle this") trigger positive feelings, whereas negative thoughts (e.g., "Nothing ever works out for me") trigger negative feelings. There are three ways of expressing personal feelings:

1. **To act them out** ("When I'm angry, I threaten others.")

2. **To defend against them** ("Angry feelings are unacceptable, so I will mask my feelings.")

3. **To accept them** ("Anger is a natural part of my life. It's okay to feel angry when someone is abusive to me.")

Of these three choices, the passive-aggressive student has learned to *defend* against his or her angry feelings by using the defense mechanisms of denial, projection, and rationalization. Because the normal feelings of irritation, anger, and hatred are unacceptable to the student, they cannot be acknowledged openly. Instead, they are masked and expressed in passive-aggressive ways.

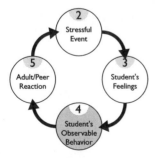

▶ Stage 4: The Student's Behavior

Personal behavior can be expressed in three ways: (1) as an automatic response (e.g., "Damn, I caught my finger in the door"), (2) as a learned response (e.g., "Thank you for the snack"), and (3) as a personal choice (e.g., "I decided to ignore his comment"). Passive-aggressive behavior most often is a learned response (e.g., "Don't show my anger") and a personal choice (i.e., "I will pretend not to hear her"). When we began our study on passive aggression, we thought most passive-aggressive behaviors were due to unconscious forces. After conferring with students and adults who are passive aggressive, we were surprised to learn how conscious and deliberate many of their acts of passive aggression were. They knew what they were doing and they seemed to enjoy the effect it had on others. They were aware of how their passive-aggressive behaviors confused and irritated others. In earlier chapters, we described these behaviors at home and in school under the following five passive-aggressive categories:

1. Temporary Compliance
2. Intentional Inefficiency
3. Letting a Problem Escalate
4. Hidden but Conscious Revenge
5. Self-Depreciation

These exasperating passive-aggressive behaviors are successful in inviting counteraggressive feelings in most adults.

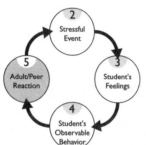

▶ **Stage 5: The Reactions of Adults**

In Chapter 7, the concept of counter–passive aggression was discussed based on the following psychological principle:

▶ In a stressful situation, a passive-aggressive student will create in the adult not only the student's feelings of anger, but also the student's passive-aggressive behaviors.

This process of behaving in counter–passive-aggressive ways develops slowly because the student's initial social behaviors are pleasant and appropriate. However, as the relationship becomes more active and personal, the student becomes frustrated and angry and behaves in passive-aggressive ways. In turn, these passive-aggressive behaviors cause the adult to experience similar feelings of anger. These feelings of anger are never discussed by the adult in the relationship but become buried and expressed in counter–passive-aggressive behaviors. When this happens, the relationship moves into a new and more painful level of interaction.

The counter–passive-aggressive behavior of the adult creates new stress for the student, causing more angry feelings and more passive-aggressive behaviors. Likewise, the adult experiences more feelings of anger and counter–passive-aggressive behaviors. This silent interpersonal passive-aggressive struggle can continue for weeks, months, or years, but ultimately the adult cannot contain the anger anymore and explodes by having a brief, intense temper tantrum. Most adults we interviewed who were in passive-aggressive relationships described their temper tantrums and were surprised by the intensity of the outbursts. We believe these temper tantrums did not happen by chance or because the adult was emotionally unstable and lacked self-control skills. These adult temper tantrums are a predictable part of the psychology of passive aggression.

The Unconscious Accumulation of Counteraggressive Feelings in an Adult

Over time, the adult unconsciously accumulates counteraggressive feelings toward a passive-aggressive student, the counteraggressive feelings increase in intensity, and the feelings erupt in a spontaneous outburst of aggression toward the student. The infamous water torture is an appropriate analogy to use to explain this process.

The water torture was devised as a method of driving a prisoner insane. By experiencing the endless drip, drip, drip of water on his or her forehead, the victim is driven into a state of madness in a few days. Each droplet of water by itself is harmless and tolerable. Each droplet of water does not cause any psychological or physical harm. But if the water droplets are continuous, they will become intolerable and will plunge the victim into screaming lunacy. This analogy is extreme, but it serves to demonstrate what happens to adults over time when they are involved in relationships with students' passive-aggressive behavior.

Figure 8.3 uses another analogy—a water faucet dripping into a jar—to depict the long-term effects of a student's passive aggression on an adult's temper. Over time, the water fills the jar until it cannot contain any more water and ends up flooding the area. We cannot overemphasize the importance of understanding that the adult is unaware of the accumulation of counteraggressive feelings toward the student. As time passes, these hidden angry feelings move from irritation to sarcasm (Times 1 and 2), to counter–passive-aggressive behavior (Time 3), to counteraggressive feelings (Time 4), to the breaking point (Time 5).

At the breaking point, the adult experiences yet one more passive-aggressive behavior from the student (e.g., "I didn't hear you. You need to speak louder"). This minor passive-aggressive behavior becomes the final act

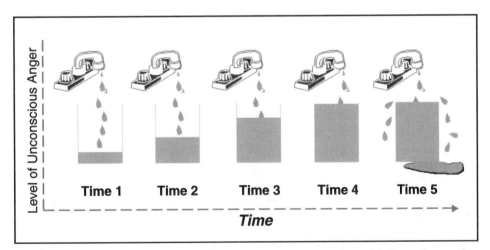

FIGURE 8.3. The accumulation over time of unconscious anger toward the student with a passive-aggressive personality. *Note.* From *The Angry Smile: Understanding and Managing Passive Aggressive Behavior of Students and Staff,* by N. J. Long, October 1998, paper presented at the Conflict Cycle Paradigm, KidsPeace National Center for Kids in Crisis, 16th National Conference, Allendale, PA. Copyright 1998 by KidsPeace. Reprinted with permission.

that floods the adult's capacity to control the counteraggressive feelings. The adult's self-control dam breaks, and all the angry feelings accumulated toward the student over the past weeks or months come flooding out in a cascade of emotional and irrational behavior. The adult yells, screams, threatens, swears, or hits the student. This reaction is a predictable and logical outcome when one is living with or teaching a passive-aggressive person. Because the adult is unaware of the unconscious accumulation of counter–passive-aggressive feelings toward the passive-aggressive student, this reaction will be repeated time and time again.

Student's Justification of Own Behavior After Adult's Tantrum

After the adult has a temper tantrum, the passive-aggressive student often responds by questioning the adult's emotional stability. Typical student comments include the following:

- "I don't know why you got so angry. All I did was say I will clean it up later."

- "It was a minor comment. I didn't yell, swear, hit, or break anything. But what you did was scary. I don't like to have someone blow up at me."

- "I don't deserve to be yelled at. I think you overreacted to this situation and mistreated me. Don't you believe you owe me an apology?"

- "I'm going to tell the principal how you verbally abused me!"

The adult, who already is feeling guilty about the temper tantrum, feels terrible and usually ends up apologizing to the student. When this happens, the student reluctantly accepts the apology on the condition that the adult will control his or her anger in the future. The adult usually agrees to these conditions, and this destructive interpersonal relationship continues until the adult's next explosive incident in a week, a month, or some future time.

The Tantrum's Validation of the Student's Self-Fulfilling Prophecy About Expression of Anger

As discussed previously, the normal expression of anger for a passive-aggressive student is a major source of anxiety because the student has never made friends with his or her normal feelings of anger. Anger in any form is perceived as a dangerous and destructive emotion that must be under control. The student perceives the expression of direct aggression as unacceptable and deserving of punishment. Once the adult explodes in anger, the temper tantrum provides the student with the visual evidence that he or she is fortunate to have his or her anger under control. The student feels absolved from any wrongdoings and has no reason to give up his or her passive-aggressive way of relating to others. In fact, the adult's temper tantrum succeeds in reinforcing the student's irrational beliefs about how dangerous it is to express anger and the importance of hiding it.

Overview of the Dynamics of Passive Aggression

To summarize the destructive interpersonal sequence of the Passive-Aggressive Conflict Cycle, between an adult and a student who is passive-aggressive, we provide the following outline:

1. Initially, the adult is attracted to the student because of his or her social skills and nonaggressive manner.

2. As the relationship experiences a normal amount of frustration, the student begins to express anger toward the adult in an indirect and subtle drip-by-drip manner, such as by not hearing, by forgetting, by procrastinating, and so on.

3. The adult becomes irritated and confused by the student's behavior and begins to mirror the student's passive-aggressive behavior by becoming counter–passive aggressive. However, the adult is unaware of the amount of anger he or she is absorbing and accumulating from the student. Over time, the adult's

(continues)

---

tolerance toward the student diminishes. Like a water glass filled to the top, the adult is loaded psychologically and ready to spill over emotionally.

4. The next time the adult makes a reasonable request and the student does not answer, burps, malingers, or sulks, the adult explodes emotionally. This insignificant but irritating behavior by the student becomes the final drip that spills the water, the spark that lights the fuse, the straw that breaks the camel's back, the pin that bursts the balloon.

5. Suddenly, the adult experiences a 30-second temper tantrum. During this time, the adult yells, screams, throws things, cusses, or even slaps the student.

6. The student reacts to the adult's aggressive behavior with shock and alarm and thinks, "Wow! Look how crazy people get when they express their anger directly. I can't believe she is so angry and out of control over such an insignificant incident! Isn't it fortunate I have learned a more effective way of controlling my anger so my anger does not control me!"

7. Once the adult has calmed down, he or she usually feels very upset and guilty for overreacting to such a minor incident. The adult not only feels sorry for losing all semblance of self-control but also thinks, "I'm a terrible person. What is wrong with me?"

8. Simultaneously, the student tells the adult that he or she does not deserve to be victimized, that the adult's behavior was an overreaction to a minor incident, and that he or she deserves an immediate apology.

9. The adult agrees and apologizes to the student by saying, "I don't know what came over me. I'm sorry. It won't happen again."

10. This apology has a special psychological meaning to the student. It reinforces the student's belief that the expression of anger is dangerous and destructive. Consequently, the student has no motivation to alter his or her passive-aggressive way of life.

11. Sadly the adult continues the emotional roller-coaster bond with the student until the next temper tantrum occurs.

This pattern of behavior will perpetuate itself until the adult is aware of his or her accumulated anger and can find appropriate ways of expressing that anger in nontoxic ways.

EXAMPLES OF THE PASSIVE-AGGRESSIVE CONFLICT CYCLE AT SCHOOL AND HOME

The following is a typical example of this passive-aggressive cycle. The teacher is a caring and compassionate person who becomes programmed by a 6-year-old passive-aggressive student named Mario. Notice how the teacher's behavior follows this sequence and how she inadvertently empowers Mario to become more passive aggressive by telling the class that they will not be able to leave or have their recess until Mario completes his task. The original intent was to put group pressure on Mario, but what she did was to turn over control of the class to Mario. Finally she explodes, grabs Mario, and then feels guilty. Even though this example takes place in a school with a young student, this pattern exists with all ages and in all settings.

Damn, my dam broke

Children affect teachers in a variety of ways. Some are precocious, yet appealing. Some are shy and introverted, yet appealing. And some do everything wrong, yet somehow there exists a special affection between teacher and child. Mario, a 6-year-old with a learning disability, did not fit into any of these categories. The only way I can describe Mario is by using the terms inconsistent and "frumpy." Yet the more I observed him, the more intellectually capable I realized he was. However, Mario never quite got all of the directions straight or completed a task "in toto." When I questioned him about his lack of concentration, he would give me a half smile that would just about send me through the ceiling. It was incredible the way Mario got under my skin. When he was messing around, I wouldn't lose my temper; I would merely say to the rest of the group, "We can't go out to recess until Mario finishes his lesson." Everyone would look back at Mario and groan. Writing about this makes me feel even more guilty than I felt then, because at that time I could defensively justify my reasons for doing something so counter–passive aggressive.

Mario and I had successive incidents, and we learned to play the game of passive aggression quite well. However, I was unaware that my hostility and anger were mounting day by day. The seepage continued through November, and one day in December it exploded!

It happened like this. At 2:35, the children were asked to go quietly for their coats, line up, and be out of the door at 2:45. Mario was always the last one to get his coat. There were many times when he would give me a half smile and tell me he couldn't find his coat. My most common answer was to ask another child, for example, "Mary, since Mario is unable to *recognize* his own coat, would you find it for him so that we can leave?" My tone would be incredibly sarcastic. Again, the children would groan. On this particular Monday, I was in a hurry to have the children leave because I had an exam scheduled at 5:00 at American University. I am sure the children sensed my haste, because I would tell them about my graduate classes, tests, papers, and so on. At 2:40, everyone had their coats on and were lined up . . . except Mario. He was sitting reading a book. I couldn't believe it! I called sternly, "Mario, go get your coat!" He looked up at me with his half smile as though I was speaking Chinese. I started to march to his seat with steam pouring out of me, but I stopped and had the presence of mind to dismiss the group. "Mario, for God's sake get your coat!" I screamed. My voice was angry, and my teeth were clenched as I spoke. He continued to look at me as if I was crazy, seemingly not understanding. Finally I grabbed him by the arm and applied pressure, as I pulled him toward the coat rack. He began to whimper. At that point I couldn't decide whether I wanted to smack him or comfort him. I did experience tremendous sorrow for the both of us and released the grip on his arm and placed my hand gently around his head as he sobbed. I had acted on my feelings and not on a professional level. I was more concerned about my needs than trying to help Mario meet his needs.

In the next example, the Passive-Aggressive Conflict Cycle takes place in the home.

This was not a good day for me

I was preparing for a dinner party one evening for my husband's boss. I worked all day getting the house and table looking beautiful, and organizing a fancy dinner. I had most everything under control until my son, Alex, age 15, and my daughter, Bethany, age 17, arrived home from school. Alex was in his typical passive-aggressive mood. He walked in and dumped his jacket on the floor. I clearly stated, "Alex, please hang up your coat pronto. I'm having Dad's boss and wife for dinner and have picked up the house all day." Alex replied, "In a minute, I'm dying of thirst," as he rushed to the spotless kitchen and opened the refrigerator, taking out a large bottle of Coke, the jelly, peanut butter, and bread. I watched in dismay as he spilled Coke and splattered crumbs across the counter and as he carried his messy snack to the breakfast nook but I said little as my growing son needed fuel. As he slowly finished eating, I said, "Okay, Alex, clean up your mess now." He replied, "Sure, sure, just as soon as I go to the bathroom." There he tarried until I had to knock and request his immediate help.

Alex was sulking and carrying his unfinished Coke as he opened the door. He placed the dripping glass on a pile of homework abandoned in the kitchen by Bethany. The glass produced a huge wet ring on Bethany's research report and I screamed, "No, not there, you idiot." He looked at me in a perplexed way, and asked, "Why do you get so angry over little things? What kind of mother are you, some kind of witch?" I then lost it completely and slapped Alex across the cheek. He was stunned and said, "I don't need your abuse." With tears of guilt and a shaky hand, I dialed my husband's office and told him about the upsetting series of events. My husband was not very sympathetic. He said, "Gosh, Ann, all he needed was some food and the bathroom after school. That doesn't sound so unreasonable to me. You seem to have overreacted to his behavior." I hung up and went to my bathtub for bubbles and a good cry.

In the previous two examples of the Passive-Aggressive Conflict Cycle, the teacher and the mother were unaware of the psychology of passive aggression and they were programmed to behave toward Mario and Alex in a predictable, no-win sequence. Once their counteraggressive feelings exploded into impulsive and inappropriate behavior, the conflict escalated into a no-win situation that included feeling guilty for their atypical aggressive outbursts. These two examples are classical descriptions of how reasonable adults who have chronic relationships with students who are passive aggressive can become trapped in the dynamics of the Passive-Aggressive Conflict Cycle.

WHEN BOTH STUDENT AND ADULT HAVE PASSIVE-AGGRESSIVE PERSONALITIES

One question our seminar participants often asked was if a passive-aggressive student ever has an impulse breakthrough like the adult. Based on our experience, the answer is *almost never*, assuming the student selects as his or her target an adult who is not passive aggressive. The student is aware of his or her psychological game and receives secondary gratification by being passive aggressive. The adult who is not passive aggressive is naive and unaware of the underlying anger of the student. The adult is unable to withstand the student's passive-aggressive strategies and will end up being the victim.

The only exception to this interpretation is when *both* the student and the adult are passive aggressive. If the adult lives with the student, the playing field is tilted toward the adult. The student no longer can control the relationship. The adult is older, has more authority and status than the student, and usually has had more experience perfecting the passive-aggressive skills. Under these psychological conditions, a chronic passive-aggressive power struggle occurs between them, and over time, the outcome favors the adult. The adult will be more tenacious and powerful and create an impossible no-win situation for the student. This situation frustrates the student and precipitates an inevitable temper tantrum. In this relationship, the student, who explodes, becomes the victim of the adult.

Managing Passive-Aggressive Students

In this book, we present a new theory of passive aggression for teachers and parents. The merit of this theory will depend on our ability to translate it into effective and teachable intervention skills. Prior to this publication, there were no professional guidelines for managing passive-aggressive student behavior. Teachers and parents were on their own to do whatever they thought was helpful at the time. Probably the most frequent reaction from a frustrated adult was to yell, "Don't let me tell you again! Do it now!" The message was loud and clear, but ineffective.

Teachers and parents no longer have to rely on their authority or participate in chronic struggles with students who are passive aggressive. To improve teachers' and parents' relationships and comfort with these students, we provide specific short- and long-term intervention skills. These skills are grouped based on two outcome goals:

▶ 1. Skills for changing one's responses to a passive-aggressive student

▶ 2. Skills for changing the behavior of a passive-aggressive student

CHANGING RESPONSES TO THE PASSIVE-AGGRESSIVE STUDENT

Skill 1: Avoid Being Deceived by the Student's Passive-Aggressive Behavior

Personal insight is the most significant and effective reason for changing your reactions to a passive-aggressive student and it is based on the statement "to be forewarned is to be forearmed." Once you know in advance the characteristics of a passive-aggressive student (see Figure 9.1), you can avoid being a naive and willing victim of the student's predictable and destructive way of engaging you. Self-awareness gives you the ability to disengage from the student emotionally and avoid reinforcing the passive-aggressive behavior.

For example, if you call a child to dinner or ask a student to share a report and she does not respond, you probably will ask her again. But if you have to ask her a third time and she still does not respond, you should immediately think "passive aggressive." Simultaneously you should say, "I've just identified her as passive aggressive, and I know she is playing her psychological game. She wants me to get angry and yell at her, so it will end up being my problem and not hers. I will not participate in this unproductive passive-aggressive

- Denies anger
- Fears intimacy
- Gives out hidden, coded messages, drip by drip
- Acts pleasant one week, intolerable the next week, making you feel you're on a perpetual emotional roller coaster
- Is often charming and intelligent
- Procrastinates and gives excessive excuses
- Keeps others waiting and dangling
- Demonstrates confusing behavior: now warm, then cold
- Acts evasive and secretive at times
- Hides anger behind a mask of confusing behaviors
- Brings out temper tantrums and feelings of guilt in others

FIGURE 9.1. Some characteristics of the passive-aggressive student.

game. I know what is behind her overt behavior of deafness. It is her feelings of anger and resentment that she is unable to express to me openly."

The skills of self-awareness and self-talk are essential to changing your behavior toward a passive-aggressive student. They provide powerful insight into the student's unexpressed anger while protecting you from internalizing the student's feelings and behaviors.

Skill 2: Acknowledge Normal Feelings of Anger

Being able to acknowledge your normal feelings of anger is a cognitive self-talk skill. You need to accept feelings of anger as real, potent, and an important part of your life. You need to say "Yes" to the presence of your anger and "No" to the expression of your anger through aggressive and passive-aggressive acts. Unlike the passive-aggressive student, you can accept having the full range of feelings instead of being controlled by your feelings. The passive-aggressive student unfortunately has learned to fear his or her anger and ends up being controlled by it.

However, life is stressful and there may be times when you need help keeping your anger under control. The following self-talk strategies are proposed to help you manage your counteraggressive feelings under three different stressful situations with a passive-aggressive student.

▶ 1. **When You Know You Will Be Meeting a Passive-Aggressive Student.** This is the time to practice saying, "I will not let him push my emotional button. I know in advance what he will do to frustrate me. This will be a challenging situation but I can handle it because I am aware of his underlying anger. I will develop a definite plan and scripted response to his passive-aggressive behaviors. Then I will know what to say and do in advance when he behaves passive aggressively. I will be in control of this situation when we meet."

▶ **2. When You Are Relating to a Passive-Aggressive Person and Are Becoming Upset.** This is the time to say to yourself, "Stop. Stay calm. Count to 15. I need to identify my feelings of anger but not become counter–passive aggressive because it will make the situation worse. I will not yell or become sarcastic because this behavior will only escalate the conflict. Remember, I am in touch with my underlying feelings of anger, and she is not. I have total choice over how I express my angry feelings in behavior. She doesn't. There is no need to doubt myself because I can see beyond her irritating passive-aggressive behavior and recognize her fear of anger. I recognize what she is trying to do to me, but I can get through it."

▶ **3. When You Are Relating to a Passive-Aggressive Person and Are About To Explode.** This is the time to say, "I know what is happening. My counteraggressive feelings are becoming intense. I need to deescalate them. If I explode, it will only reinforce his irrational beliefs about anger and make my life miserable. I will instruct myself to lower my tone and volume and to speak more slowly. I will assert myself by sending an 'I' message (e.g., I am having difficulty dealing with your behavior right now. I need to sort out my feelings. We need to discuss this situation but not right now. I need to stop this conversation but later want the opportunity to share with you my thoughts about our relationship.). Now I will walk away quickly and with confidence."

These three cognitive self-talk strategies are useful anger management skills and have four personal advantages:

1. They will stop the accumulation of unconscious anger that we discussed in Chapter 7.

2. They will prevent you from having an emotional meltdown when your unconscious anger would have erupted.

3. They will protect you from your subsequent feelings of guilt if you had an emotional temper tantrum.

4. They will eliminate the expression of your aggressive behavior that the student uses to justify his behavior and his belief that the expression of anger is dangerous.

Skill 3: Stop All Counter–Passive-Aggressive Behaviors

The Passive-Aggressive Conflict Cycle demonstrates how the student's passive-aggressive behaviors create in adults not only the student's angry feelings, but also his or her identical passive-aggressive behaviors. Remember, the adult rarely initiates the Passive-Aggressive Conflict Cycle, but often the adult behaves in a way to perpetuate it. Once this happens, the adult needs to stop all the "you" messages that promote counter–passive-aggressive behaviors. For example, the adult needs to verbalize an I message (e.g., "I am becoming upset and need to stop and understand why I am feeling angry. Perhaps this is something you need to think about too.").

Skill 4: Avoid Empowering a Passive-Aggressive Person

When frustrated by a passive-aggressive student, never empower her by giving her control of the situation. Never say to other children at home, "We can't go to the movie until Norma feeds the dog." And never say to a class, "Everyone will have to stop all activity until Leroy gets off the floor." In each of these examples, the adult inadvertently gives the passive-aggressive student the power to control the situation and influence the immediate comfort and pleasure of others.

The original intent of these comments was to create group pressure on Norma and Leroy to get them to conform. However, the passive-aggressive student may think, "Thank you, now I can delay and procrastinate and frustrate the whole group." Consequently, instead of solving the problem, the adult has escalated the problem. If, however, you have already made the mistake of empowering the passive-aggressive student, you can change your mind and say, "I have thought it over and I've decided to change my mind. We can all go, but Leroy will have to stay." This immediately reestablishes the power and control from the student to the adult.

CHANGING STUDENTS' PASSIVE-AGGRESSIVE BEHAVIORS

Skill 5: Use Benign Confrontation as a Long-Term Effective Intervention

When we began this study of passive aggression, we believed that most of students' passive-aggressive behaviors were driven by hidden and unconscious feelings of anger and hatred. We believed that these students used unconscious defense mechanisms, such as denial, rationalization, projection, and displacement. After talking with hundreds of passive-aggressive children and adults over the years, however, we have changed our view. We are convinced that the majority of passive-aggressive behaviors are consciously motivated, and that only a small percentage are unconsciously motivated. The only exception to this interpretation is that most passive-aggressive students involved in self-depreciation are unaware of the underlying forces that motivate their dysfunctional behavior. As a result, they need more professional help than a Benign Confrontation provides. Excluding this group of students, we believe that most passive-aggressive students know what they are doing, are aware of their anger, and think that others are unaware of their covert anger. We found, for example, that when students are confronted about their passive-aggressive behavior, they usually respond by saying, "I don't know what you're talking about." But if we simultaneously observe their nonverbal behavior when we confront them, a different message usually emerges. They often give a half-smile, shift their eyes, or cock their heads in a revealing way. This lets us know our comment about their behavior was true. A few passive-aggressive persons, much to our surprise, have told us privately and with delightful satisfaction how enjoyable, rewarding, and effective it is to be passive aggressive. It appears that a passive-aggressive person receives an abundant amount of self-reinforcing pleasure from the passive-aggressive behavior.

Benign Confrontation is the only technique we have found to be successful in changing the behavior of a passive-aggressive student by identifying his or her underlying anger. Benign Confrontation is a verbal intervention skill in which the adult gently but openly shares his or her thoughts about the student's behavior and unexpressed anger. It is based on the decision not to silently accept the student's manipulative and controlling behavior any longer. The effectiveness of Benign Confrontation is contingent on using knowledge of the passive-aggressive personality. The following is an outline of how to use the skill of Benign Confrontation:

1. Recognize how frustrating it is to teach and live with a student who is chronically passive aggressive.

2. Realize that the student has a toxic reaction to any criticism about his or her behavior, whether it comes from a family member, teacher, friend, acquaintance, or stranger. Benign Confrontation is not an aggressive, in-your-face adversarial skill, but a quiet, reflective skill.

3. Share with the student your awareness that the difficulty you are having in the relationship is the student's reluctance to talk about his or her anger. Benign Confrontation is the skill of gently dropping a pebble of a new idea into the student's static pool of thought.

4. When the student denies the role that his or her anger plays in the relationship or claims that you have misunderstood him or her, respond, "Okay! It was just a thought I wanted to share with you." Do not argue or correct the student's denial at this time but quietly back away from further discussion and leave the student with the thought that you are aware there are some feelings of anger behind his or her behavior. The advantage of Benign Confrontation is the comfort of not having to justify or defend your shared observations about the student's underlying anger. By telling the student you are aware of his or her covert anger, you are sending a message that this relationship needs to change. The effectiveness of Benign Confrontation begins after the student's initial denial of your observations of his or her covert anger. The student may deny it verbally, but he or she knows that his or her anger is not a private secret anymore. Like a pebble dropped into a pool, the ripple effect of Benign Confrontation goes beyond the student's initial surprise that you have identified the anger underlying the passive-aggressive behavior. Your revelation also takes away the secondary pleasure the student receives from being passive aggressive. More important, the student knows that you have opened the door for future discussion about his or her passive-aggressive behavior and underlying anger.

5. After identifying another clear example of the student's passive-aggressive behavior, share your thoughts about his or her behavior and under-

lying anger. For example, you might say, "I just had a thought I want to share with you. What just happened between us reminded me of a previous problem we had last week. Remember when I mentioned I thought you were angry at me? Well, this incident seems similar to that incident. What do you think?" Again, do not argue the point, but leave the student with this thought to reverberate in his or her mind.

6. After several more opportunities of using Benign Confrontation, move to the next level. This time, when you observe another example of passive-aggressive behavior, respond, "Guess what I am going to say about this behavior?" or "What do you think I am going to say next?" The student's typical answer is, "You probably are going to talk about my anger." This statement is an important acknowledgment of the change in the relationship. The student knows he or she cannot hide behind the rationalization (e.g., by saying, "I forgot, I didn't hear you," "I didn't understand what you wanted"). Also, the student is no longer getting secondary pleasure from passive-aggressive behavior and now considers Benign Confrontation as a painful anxiety-provoking experience he or she wants to avoid. The student faces two choices: to change the passive-aggressive behavior or to be benignly confronted by the adult again and again.

> Benign Confrontation is the skill of building an emotional fire in the passive-aggressive student without having him or her boil over in protest.

Example of Benign Confrontation

The following example of a 12-year-old student and her teacher is presented to demonstrate how Benign Confrontation can be used successfully with a passive-aggressive student.

Put the cards in the box, please

Sarah is a smart, attractive 12-year-old who attends an alternative school. She is a delightful girl whenever she is in control of an activity. Sarah was involved in a remedial writing lesson and was asked by her teacher to stop and put the cards in the box so they could begin her math lesson. The box was in front of Sarah. Sarah didn't respond, and the teacher asked again. Sarah didn't respond the second, third, or fourth time, causing the teacher's voice to go up a few decibels. By the fifth request, the teacher was aware that Sarah heard her but was being silently oppositional. The teacher simultaneously gave herself this message: "This is a reasonable request and this girl is not going to win, and I'm not going to back down. She will put the cards in the box!" Now the Passive-Aggressive Conflict Cycle was in full swing. Sarah was clearly angry on the inside but smiled and looked pleasantly confused on the outside. The teacher now was mirroring Sarah's behavior. She was angry on the inside but being sweet on the outside by repeating, "Please, put the cards in the box! You can put the cards away." Finally, "Put the cards away, Sarah!" Sarah continued to be passive and smiled for the next 20 minutes without saying a word. The teacher was furious but there were no winners in this passive-aggressive stalemate.

Using the concept of Benign Confrontation to change Sarah's behavior

To use Benign Confrontation, the teacher needs to understand the psychology of passive aggression and be able to control her counteraggressive feelings toward Sarah. The following are the steps the teacher needs to learn to help Sarah:

1. After the second request to put the cards away, the teacher should have identified Sarah as passive aggressive and said to herself, "Sarah is being passive aggressive and I will not participate in her strategy."

2. The teacher should share her thoughts about Sarah's underlying anger. The teacher should say calmly, "Sarah, let's stop. I have a thought I want to share with you. I asked you to put away the cards, and you pretended not to hear me. I know I speak clearly, and other students can hear me easily. What I have to figure out is why, at this particular time, you are choosing not to hear me and follow my reasonable request. (Pause. No response from Sarah.) My guess is that a part of you may be upset with me. You probably would prefer to continue to write than do math right now. If so, we need to talk about your anger and stop pretending you can't hear me. Sarah, the difficulty we are having right now is not about the cards. We can forget about the cards and who puts them away. What is happening between us right now is important. Perhaps, we may have discovered a pattern of behavior you use when you are angry. (Pause.) Perhaps, when I ask you to do something you think is not fair or pleasurable, you act as if you don't hear me. Sarah, you are a smart student, so let me hear what you think about this situation."

3. After this Benign Confrontation, which exposes Sarah's hidden anger, Sarah's first response is to refuse to talk or to deny it. At this time, the teacher should back off and not persist. If Sarah refuses to discuss the incident, the teacher should say, "It is difficult to talk about personal issues but I want you to *think* about it." If Sarah says there is no problem, the teacher should say, "I'm glad you believe this is not a problem. In other words, if I ask you to do something like put the cards away, you will be willing to do it?" If Sarah agrees, then once again the teacher should ask her to put the cards in the box. However, a new level of insight has developed between Sarah and her teacher. This process of Benign Confrontation will change the way Sarah and her teacher think about each other in the future. Sarah's passive-aggressive behavior no longer is a secret and effective technique of getting back at the adults in her life.

4. Each time the teacher identifies a clear example of Sarah's passive-aggressive behavior, the teacher will use the skill of Benign Confrontation to identify Sarah's underlying anger.

Benign Confrontation is the skill we recommend to use with students and family members who resort to temporary deafness, feign misunderstanding, procrastinate, and are intentionally inefficient. Using Benign Confrontation is like building a mosaic in which multiple parts must be connected before the picture has meaning. The good news is Benign Confrontation works!

Skill 6: Respond Differently to Passive-Aggressive Temporary Deafness—The Detective Colombo Technique

Short-Term Approach

This is an effective skill to use in the classroom during group activities. When you identify a passive-aggressive student who is feigning temporary deafness, we suggest using the Detective Colombo technique. After three requests with no response, walk up to the student, look at the ceiling, and express your thoughts in a soft voice, as if you were talking to yourself but so he can hear you. Say, "Isn't this interesting? I asked Sam to get the book off the table, and he pretended he didn't hear me. I know he can hear. I think I'll ask him one more time and see what he does." Then look Sam straight in the eyes and say, "Sam, will you please get me the encyclopedia, letter M, from the back of the room?"

In 90% of cases, the student will complete the task immediately. By exposing his mask of temporary deafness, Sam is more likely to respond positively than if you continue to escalate your demands. In talking with passive-aggressive students, they have shared with us their belief that "adults are naive and stupid, and it is easy to trick them into believing we don't hear them." Detective Colombo appears naive and stupid, but his laid-back, pondering technique is unusually effective in letting the opponents know that he knows what they are doing.

Long-Term Approach

Wait for an undebatable example of a student's feigning deafness and use Benign Confrontation.

Skill 7: Respond Differently to Passive-Aggressive Feigned Misunderstanding

Short-Term Approach

Feigned misunderstanding masks passive aggression behind a veil of sincerity. When you ask your son to cut the grass and he goes outside only to return an hour later without completing this chore, do not be surprised if he says, "I didn't understand you wanted me to do it right away." When you tell a passive-aggressive student her report has to be 10 pages and she hands in 3 pages and says, "I was sure you said the report only had to be 3 pages," do not be surprised. These examples illustrate how the student can justify passive-aggressive behavior by feigning misunderstanding. "I forgot!" is also a frequent excuse from this type of student.

The skill of managing this type of passive-aggressive behavior is to set clear expectations. *Never* assume that passive-aggressive students understand your request. One way to make them accountable is to review your requests with them or give them the requests in writing. In most cases, this will help, but unless you also talk about their underlying anger, improved results will be only temporary.

Long-Term Approach

Wait for an undebatable example of a student's feigned misunderstanding and use Benign Confrontation.

Skill 8: Respond Differently to Passive-Aggressive Delay Behaviors

Short-Term Approach

Passive-aggressive delay behavior is defined as procrastination in which the student expresses hidden anger by slowing down and responding in sluggish ways. When you ask your son to clean his room, and he says, "Don't worry, I'll clean it sometime this morning," or when you ask a student if she has completed her book report, and she answers, "I'll do it after I read this chapter," the underlying feeling of anger is expressed as "Why should I do it for you?"

Setting precise limits and deadlines with a clear, natural consequence is helpful, but the change will be only temporary. For example, when you say to your son, "Okay, let's agree you will clean up your room by noon. If you do it, you can go to the mall. If you don't, you choose to stay home until it is completed." You can tell your student, "Let's agree your report will be completed by the end of this period. If you do it, you are free to follow your schedule. If you don't, you choose to write the report in the study hall during recess." In these examples, the goal is to make the student and not the adult responsible for the student's behavior.

Long-Term Approach

Wait for an undebatable example of the student's passive-aggressive delay behavior and use Benign Confrontation.

Skill 9: Respond Differently to Passive-Aggressive Chronically Late Behavior

Short-Term Approach

A student who is habitually late coming home, arriving at school, and attending scheduled activities because of passive-aggressive behavior, is indirectly expressing anger toward these activities or people by keeping them waiting. Habitual lateness not only frustrates others but also provides the student with secondary gratification by thinking, "Ha, ha, I don't have to meet your expectations," or "My time is more important than your time." The skill of dealing with this type of behavior, once again, includes setting clear limits with the student and taking away any secondary gratification the person may receive by being late.

When you tell your teenager to be home on Friday night by 11:00 and she arrives home at midnight, do not argue with her or get into a long discussion about her excuses for being late. Say, "You decided not to be home at the agreed-upon time and therefore we are choosing for you to come home at 10:30 next weekend." This is one of the few times where any further discussion with the teenager will only lead to an increased power struggle. Remember to follow through with limits.

Long-Term Approach

Wait for an undebatable example of the student's passive-aggressive late behavior and use Benign Confrontation.

Skill 10: Evaluate Your Own Personality

Evalutating one's own personality is not an easy or comfortable skill to learn because a person is usually the last to learn about the impact of his or her behavior on others. This skill begins by looking in a mirror and asking yourself if you are a passive-aggressive personality or are reacting to authority figures in a passive-aggressive way. If the answer is "Yes," you have identified one source of your conflictual relationships with others. We recommend that you seek professional help with a psychotherapist who can help you understand the etiology of your passive-aggressive personality, and the role that anger plays in your life.

In addition, you also need to complete a comprehensive course on anger management to learn how to redirect your anger from passive-aggressive behaviors to assertive behaviors.

CLOSING COMMENT

We hope that, after reading this book, you find the study of passive aggression to be an exciting psychological adventure that changes the way you think, feel, and behave toward a passive-aggressive student. You now understand the hidden mystery of passive aggression and can avoid being lured into a future and painful passive-aggressive relationship. You have the knowledge to change your responses to a student's passive-aggressive behavior and have learned an effective intervention skill called Benign Confrontation. As you practice these skills, you will become more comfortable and confident talking about the unexpressed anger in your relationships. The psychology of passive aggression provides the knowledge and skills to teach and live with a student who is passive aggressive in a different and more satisfying way . . . assuming you don't procrastinate.

References

Burns, D. (1991). *Feeling good*. New York: Avon Books.

Long, J., & Long, N. (1996). Understanding and managing the passive aggressive student. In N. Long & W. Morse (Eds.), *Conflict in the classroom* (5th ed., pp. 352–361). Austin, TX: PRO-ED.

Long, N. J. (1996). The conflict cycle paradigm on how troubled students get teachers out of control. In N. Long & W. Morse (Eds.), *Conflict in the classroom* (5th ed., pp. 244–264). Austin, TX: PRO-ED.

Long, N. J. (1998, October). *The angry smile: Understanding and managing passive aggressive behavior of students and staff*. Paper presented at the Conflict Cycle Paradigm, KidsPeace National Center for Kids in Crisis, 16th National Conference, Allendale, PA.

Rosenfeld, M. (1997, November 10). Daddy severest. *Washington Post*, p. B1.

Silver, L. (1992). *Dr. Larry Silver's advice to parents on attention-deficit hyperactivity disorder*. Washington, DC: American Psychiatric Press.

Smith, S. (1992). *Succeeding against the odds*. Los Angeles: Jeremy P. Tarcher.

U.S. Department of Education. (1999). *National center for education statistics*. Washington, DC: Author. Retrieved from the World Wide Web: www.nces.ed.gov/pubs2001/034b.pbs

Wetzler, S. (1992, October 12). Sugarcoated hostility. *Newsweek Magazine*, p. 14.

About the Authors

Dr. Nicholas J. Long is a national leader in teaching and programming for emotionally disturbed children and youth. He received his PhD in human development from the University of Michigan in 1957 and was on the faculty of Indiana University, Georgetown University Department of Psychiatry, and The American University, where he is professor emeritus. He is a licensed clinical psychologist and was chief of the Children's Treatment Center at the NIMH, executive director of Hillcrest Children's Psychiatry Center in Washington, DC, and founder of The Rose School, a therapeutic day treatment program for troubled students. He has co-authored *Conflict in the Classroom* (5th ed.), *Teaching Children Self Control,* and *Life Space Intervention.* Currently he is co-editor of *Reclaiming Children and Youth: The Journal of Strength Based Interventions* and president of the Life Space Crisis Intervention Institute.

Dr. Jody Long is a licensed school psychologist who served for many years in the District of Columbia school system. She received her BS in education at Indiana University, was a sixth-grade teacher in Schenectady, New York, and obtained a MA in educational psychology from Indiana University. She received her PhD in counseling psychology from The American University and served as coordinator of The American University–Rose School Program while serving as an active board member in her children's schools. She co-authored *Conflict and Comfort in College* and professional articles on adolescents. Currently, she is president of The Institute of Psychoeducational Training and is in private practice.